BACH FLOWER REMEDIES:
DIAGNOSIS AND TREATMENT

DAVID LORD

Dr. Edward Bach, a British physician who practiced during the first decades of the 20th century, realized that treating the *symptoms* of an illness did not necessarily treat the *cause* of the illness. After studying homeopathy and pharmacology, he concentrated on flowers and came up with a package of 38 flower remedies for a wide range of physical and emotional conditions. This book presents the 38 remedies, with a description of each one, its aims and its results; in this way, it teaches the reader to diagnose and decide upon the appropriate treatment. More importantly, the book recounts dozens of actual cases which have been successfully treated with Bach Flower Remedies.

David Lord was born in Scotland. From childhood, he suffered from asthma. After graduating from university, he moved to London and became acquainted with holistic healing. He was immediately drawn to Bach Flower Remedies, the only method that was successful in curing his lifelong struggle with asthma. Lord now lives in the Far East. He is involved in a special project that will produce remedies derived from Himalayan flowers. This is his first book.

ASTROLOG - THE HEALING SERIES

Holistic Healing
Rachel Lewin

Feng Shui
Richard Taylor and Wang Tann

Reiki
Bill Waites and Master Naharo

Bach Flower Remedies
David Lord

Aromatherapy
Marion Wayman

Reflexology
Nathan B. Strauss

Shiatsu
Nathan B. Strauss

BACH FLOWER REMEDIES

DIAGNOSIS AND TREATMENT

David Lord

Astrolog Publishing House

P. O. Box 1123, Hod Hasharon 45111, Israel
Tel: 972-9-7412044
Fax: 972-9-7442714
E-Mail: info@astrolog.co.il
Astrolog Web Site: www.astrolog.co.il

ISBN 965-494-058-2

Published by Astrolog Publishing House 1999

Printed in Israel
10 9 8 7 6 5 4 3 2 1

INTRODUCTION

Dr. Edward Bach was born in Britain in 1886. He studied traditional medicine, and qualified as a general practitioner. Like most GPs of the time, Dr. Bach treated a large number of patients every day. Over the years of his experience, he began to notice that certain symptoms were more prevalent at certain times; for example, there were more headaches, colds, stomach-aches, and so on just after pay-day, on Monday mornings, before the due date for the payment of taxes, etc.

Dr. Bach listened to what his patients had to say, and he would administer the appropriate treatment for the particular symptoms of which the patient was complaining. The patient would get relief from pain and discomfort, but Dr. Bach realized that he was not getting to the root of the problem: The cause of the illness was not really being treated - only the side-effects.

He made the revolutionary connection between state of mind and state of body, realizing that the person's emotional state has a direct influence on his physical condition. In fact, it is the main cause of most ailments. Therefore, the correct treatment would be to eradicate the cause of the problem, which is usually in the mind. He likened treating symptoms to a thorn stuck in the flesh, and treating the resulting infection without removing the thorn itself from the flesh, so that the infection inevitably recurs over and over again. He concluded that he had to locate the trigger that could change the person's emotional state.

In order to apply his radical theory, he studied pharmacology and homeopathy so as to understand the use of plants and flowers in medicine. He specialized in flowers, classifying them according to how they influenced a number of emotional states which were responsible for causing numerous ailments. At first, he came up with a set of twelve extracts which he called "The Twelve Healers." He called other plant extracts "remedies."

Dr. Bach spent years researching flower and plant extracts, and finally, during the early 1930s, came up with a package of 38 flower extracts (numbered according to their alphabetical order) that he divided into seven categories, each of which was aimed at treating the manifestations of a particular emotional disorder which was responsible for causing physical diseases. He gave specific instructions for the diagnosis of diseases, and the preparation and administration of the remedies.

Dr. Bach also prepared what he called a "rescue package" consisting of a combination of five extracts, for emergency use.

The remedies are not in the least dangerous to health, and can be used in combination with no deleterious effects. The usual dose is 2-4 drops diluted in pure water, taken three times a day. The extracts can also be massaged directly into the skin.

In this book, the Bach Flower Remedies are presented according to Dr. Bach's original division of the remedies into categories. Each category is laid out as follows:

In the title, the number of the extract appears. If there is an asterisk, it means that the extract is one of Dr. Bach's original "Twelve Healers."

The second line gives the common name of the remedy.

The third line indicates the color of the remedy - this color is also suitable for color therapy.

At the end of the book (on pages 158 and 159), there is a complete list of all the extracts in their categories. Following this is a list (on page 160) of all the extracts in their numerical order.

Extracts for the Treatment of Fears

Extract 20*

Mimulus

Yellow

Aims to change: shyness, fear deriving from a known source (such as acrophobia - fear of heights, hydrophobia - fear of water, etc.).

Improves: courage to confront fears, ability to function despite the fear.

Fear of the Decorator

At the age of six, Sally was a normal child with normal behavioral patterns. She had never experienced any particular anxieties or fears, other than the characteristic ones displayed by children of her age group, such as fear of the dark. Before Easter, her parents decided to have the apartment decorated. The painter who came to the apartment to do the work was a large, swarthy, heavily-built man. He had a round face and a double chin, and his eyes were slightly slanted. He would generally turn up for work unshaven, and dressed in shabby work clothes covered with paint stains. The decorator greeted Sally every morning when he arrived for work, but the looks he gave her always frightened her, and she would scurry away to a corner of the kitchen, peering out at him in terror, almost anguish. She was not an outgoing child, and did not confide her fears or anxieties to anyone. Her mother apparently interpreted Sally's behavior as simple shyness.

Toward the end of the week, the painter began to decorate the next-door apartment where Sally's aunt lived. However, not only did Sally's nightmares not cease - they continued for another week. During that time, Sally's hair began to fall out, and every morning there would be strands of hair on her pillow, and her hairbrush was full of hair after each brushing.

After Sally's mother managed to persuade her daughter to tell her why she was scared, Sally was treated with Mimulus extract. In addition to drops that she put in Sally's drinking water, Sally's mother also massaged her scalp with the extract. Sally stopped shedding hair within a week of starting the treatment.

Anna's Drowning Trauma

Anna, a woman in her forties, experienced a serious trauma in her childhood during a visit to the seaside with her family. The incident occurred when she was 11. Although she did not know how to swim, she went into the sea, which appeared calm, with the intention of splashing around in shallow water. As she entered the water, however, a large wave rushed in and washed her out to sea. Anna was caught up in the wave and began to swallow sea-water. She thrashed around hysterically and thought the end had come. Luckily, a man who happened to be swimming nearby immediately pulled her out of the water to the beach, where the lifeguard attended to her. Since that traumatic day, Anna not only suffered from a fear of the sea and swimming pools, but she developed a fear of water of all kinds. Even when she had small children of her own, she avoided washing them in a bathtub filled with water, and did not let them play in inflatable pools in the garden.

Anna's husband, who had to live with her fears, finally decided to do something about them. Anna was persuaded to try Bach flower remedies, and was treated with Mimulus mixed with White Chestnut. Just six weeks after starting the treatment, Anna was able to immerse herself in a swimming-pool - up to her knees - for the first time in many years. Eventually, she was able to go into the water up to her waist, then to her chest, until she completely overcame her fears. Today, she even knows how to swim.

The Businessman's Chronic Eye Infection

Alan was a successful businessman, who had made his fortune by sheer hard work, as well as acute business acumen. He did not have any formal training in his line of business, relying mainly on his gut instincts for assessing the chances of success of his business transactions. However, Alan suffered from unceasing anxiety - that his business would fail and all his achievements would come to naught. Occasionally, this worry would paralyze him completely, and he would have to take a day or two off from work in order to overcome the stresses and fears of which he was only too well aware. The situation became so bad that Alan eventually developed a chronic eye infection that he was unable to shake off, despite trying every remedy on the market. A friend suggested that he try a Bach flower remedy, and Alan was treated with Rock Water extract. Several weeks later, the infection disappeared entirely and his colleagues remarked that his eyes were no longer bloodshot; they wondered which health resort he had visited...

Meanwhile, Alan began to study for a degree in his field of work, and this boosted his confidence in his business dealings. Today, Alan is a successful businessman with healthy eyes, and is free of fears, anxiety and lack of confidence.

Extract 25

Red Chestnut

Red

Aims to change: sense of indebtedness to others, fear of tragedies, expecting the worst.
Improves: genuine, pure and practical concern, without hypersensitivity.

Over-Anxious About His Epileptic Girlfriend

This is a classic story of first love. Eddie was 16 when he met Hilary, his first true love. She enchanted him, not only because of her charm and her somewhat unkempt appearance, but mainly because of her wit and intelligence. She completely turned his head, and he was madly in love. He inscribed her name on his books and had T-shirts made with both their names on them. She was never out of his thoughts, and became part of his daily existence.

Hilary, however, was not like all the other girls. She suffered from epilepsy. Eddie read up on the illness until he knew everything there was to know about it. His greatest fear was that something would happen to his beloved Hilary, and that he would not be with her when she needed him. He was also worried that he could lose her as a result of an epileptic seizure. He was constantly anxious, and he started imagining horrific situations in which he might lose Hilary. He became so obsessed with his anxieties that he began to lose interest in his studies. Of course, Hilary also suffered as a result of Eddie's worries; she would have preferred him to treat her like any other girl.

Eddie's mother, who was very concerned about her son, decided to have him treated with Bach flower remedies. Eddie was treated with Red Chestnut and White

Chestnut extracts and, after four weeks, his condition improved dramatically. He became less worried about the things that could happen to Hilary, and he began to shake off his obsessive anxieties. Hilary was relieved, as Eddie's exaggerated concern for her health had been very tiresome. Eddie's schoolwork picked up and he began to relate to his classmates, something he had not done before. In short, Eddie resumed a normal life.

Anxieties that Led to Rebellion

Dorothy was a very anxious mother. Her worries about the well-being of her three children of elementary-school and kindergarten age became almost pathological. She had fussed over them from the day they were born and never let them do a thing without her being by their side. She watched over them constantly to ensure that they would not fall or trip over anything. In fact, they received very few bumps and scrapes in their early childhood, as she was always on hand to make sure nothing happened to them. Her husband's and friends' pleas that she give the children a bit of freedom fell on deaf ears. Explanations that the children would not be able to recognize danger if they never had the chance to experience it were to no avail. She would not let them learn by experience.

The eldest of the three children began to feel the burden of his mother's over-anxiety when he reached school age, and was taunted by his classmates for being the only kid in the class whose mother brought him to school every day. She even took him to play at his friends' houses in the afternoon, even if they lived next door. Everyone knew that Dorothy was always the supervising parent on any class trip. Dorothy's children often felt embarrassed by their mother's behavior. The constant pressure, first on the eldest child and then on his siblings, began to leave its mark, and the children began to rebel and demand independence.

The rebellion affected every aspect of their home life - from deciding what to wear in the morning and which breakfast cereal to eat, to endless arguments about bedtime and brushing teeth. Dorothy told her husband that she could not control her fears and exaggerated anxiety about her children's welfare. While she did it out of concern for their well-being, she was aware that she was overdoing the pressure, but she was incapable of changing. Life at home became unbearable, and Dorothy's husband, sensing that the children's rebelliousness was a reaction to their mother's behavior, decided to persuade her to get treatment.

She was treated with Red Chestnut and Chicory, and during the course of the treatment, the parents and children discussed the situation and devised a special program designed to help Dorothy conquer her fears.

Dorothy gradually began to ease the pressure on her children and allow them a greater degree of freedom and independence. They were very appreciative of the change in her, and this was reflected in the way they related to her.

Extract 2

Aspen

Brown/Green

Aims to change: fear of the unknown, psychological fears, vague and indistinct fears, fear of the future.

Improves: confidence deriving from belief that enables the person to cope with the experience of fear.

A Chicago Story

Alex had lived in Chicago all his life. He adored the city, its sights and smells, and its atmosphere. But despite his love for the city, he was adamant about moving to Southern California because of Chicago's cold winters. Every time he was caught in a powerful blizzard, he experienced unexplained fears and trepidation.

His fears would increase as the fury of the blizzard augmented, and tremors would attack his entire body, sometimes to such an extent that he would scream uncontrollably if he could not find immediate shelter from the blizzard.

Of course, Alex had no idea why this happened to him, and all his efforts to discover the source of this phobia - possibly due to some childhood trauma or some other previous experience - or to pinpoint when it had begun were to no avail. Only one thing was certain: he had no control over his reactions.

Every day throughout the winter, he would peer out of his window anxiously to see what the weather had in store for him. If the treetops were leaning precariously in the wind, Alex knew what to expect. There were days when he never left the house for fear of being caught in a blizzard. He avoided walking, and used his car to get around. On particularly cold days, he planned his route so that he was able to go straight from the parking lot at his apartment to the parking lot at his destination. Life in winter was almost unbearable for Alex. Eventually, despite his great regret at leaving the city he loved, he decided to move to a town in a warmer part of the country where there were no blizzards. However, during his search for a new town, he ran into a friend who suggested that he try his luck with Bach flower remedies.

Alex began the treatment in the late summer, before the stormy season began. He was treated with an Aspen extract, and gradually his condition began to improve. Slowly but surely, Alex began to notice that his terrible anxiety attacks and destructive feelings were diminishing, eventually disappearing altogether.

Alex no longer stares anxiously out at the treetops before deciding whether to venture outside, and he still resides happily in his beloved Chicago. He can now cope with the blizzards, although he still does not quite welcome them with open arms... The treatment had a very significant effect on his life.

Hospital Claustrophobia

Whenever Cindy entered a hospital, she experienced a feeling of claustrophobia. She felt that try as she might to expand her lungs, she simply could not get enough air to breathe. Fortunately, Cindy did not have much cause to go to hospitals - and even then it was generally only on happy occasions, such as visiting a friend or relative who had just had a baby. The problem was not too acute, and Cindy managed to survive the occasional "mini-traumas" relatively well. However, one day, after a long search, Cindy found a job as a bookkeeper - in the hospital in her home town! The job looked interesting, paid well, and offered satisfactory working conditions.

Cindy started to go to work every day, and felt claustrophobic every time she entered the hospital. The feeling was unbearable: She felt dizzy and could hardly breath, as if her trachea had closed up. The tension she felt every morning before reaching the hospital generated an even greater level of anxiety. The situation worsened. Although, once seated at her desk, the discomfort soon vanished, she never overcame the unbearable feelings that overwhelmed her every time she entered the hospital. After some time, the situation became so serious that Cindy decided to quit her job, despite her fierce desire to continue working there.

When she reached the point of desperation, help came from an unexpected quarter. One day, just before she finally decided to look for a new job, she ran into a childhood friend in the hospital corridor. When Cindy told her friend that they were fortunate to have met in the hospital, as she was about to leave her job, and confided the reasons for her decision, her friend referred her to a Bach flower practitioner. Cindy, who was skeptical by nature, doubted the efficacy of healing remedies, particularly in view of the intensity of her phobic symptoms. However, she was keen to keep her job, so she opted for Bach flower treatment. "I've got nothing to lose," she told herself.

She was treated with Aspen extract over a period of four weeks. By the first week, her symptoms had already diminished. After a few weeks, the symptoms began to disappear altogether, and, after two months, Cindy was completely cured. Today, several years later, Cindy is head of the department at the hospital and even laughs when she recalls the time she was almost forced to quit her job.

Extract 26*

Rock Rose

Yellow

Aims to change: extreme fear, hysteria, panic, nightmares.

Improves: heroic courage, selfishness or the ability to love oneself, the ability to overcome fear.

Drugs and Hallucinations

Steve had been addicted to hard drugs for two years. He came from a "good home" - both parents were academics with successful careers, and they led a comfortable life. Steve was a rich kid looking for meaning in life, and found himself spending most of his days going on trips to places to which only the hardest hallucinatory drugs could take him. His parents only discovered his drug habit late in the day. Twice they had him committed to the best and most expensive drug rehabilitation center in the country, and each time Steve managed to escape. Only when he realized he was teetering on the brink of the abyss, and was about to go over, did he decide to make a last-ditch effort to summon his last reserves of strength and kick the habit.

After a long, torturous process, which caused agony both for Steve and his family, he managed to kick the habit. He realized that he could not entirely eradicate the "disease"; it would always lurk inside him. It was a daily struggle, a never-ending battle. However, he received all the support he needed from his family and friends.

Despite resuming a normal life, Steve still suffered from monstrous nightmares that brought him back to the brink of anxiety, hysteria and despair. His nightmares were a tangible experience for Steve, full of crazy and distorted images, causing his heart to palpitate. He felt as if he were falling from a 20-story building and smashing into a million pieces on the ground. He was gripped by total panic and, after a night like that, he would get up in the morning devoid of strength to face the day ahead. The traumatic dreams would drown him in a sea of fears. The overriding feeling was one of physical exhaustion, as if he had gone ten rounds with a champion boxer, and he would stay in bed all day. He had no strength in his muscles and was unable to get out of bed and stand on his feet. He felt as if he had run out of life force, and could not get a hold of himself. He would stay in bed and cry, ending up feeling even more tired.

He underwent treatment with Rock Rose extract, which is also used as a rescue remedy. It strengthened his resolve and helped him recover. Rock Rose also helped Steve accept himself as he was, and he felt love for himself and for others around him. His sleep was calmer and his dreams, even if they were still filled with images from the past, did not induce a sense of hysteria and panic. His self-confidence was restored, and he was able to cope with reality once again, and lead a normal life.

Destructive Love

Rachel was a strong young woman, and a very dominant figure within her social circle. She was always in the thick of things, until she met Leo, and fell head over heels in love with him. Leo was a talented and creative young man, full of original ideas, and Rachel loved and admired him to the point of negating her own personality and merging into the background in his presence. He was her entire world, and she never dared argue with him or contradict him. His word was law. For his part, he had fallen in love with the girl Rachel had been before, and was now disappointed with what she had become. The relationship of total dependency was not to his liking, and eventually he broke up with her. The separation was soul-destroying for Rachel, and she was petrified of being left on her own. She was sure that she would never get over it. She was emotionally devastated, and stopped functioning: she did not eat, could not concentrate on anything, and felt devoid of spiritual strength. She lost her zest for life, and nothing interested her anymore. Her physical condition deteriorated, and she lost over 40 pounds.

Two months later, when Rachel's condition not only did not improve, but worsened, her shocked mother realized the seriousness of her daughter's condition and decided to do something about it. She knew about Bach flower remedies and referred her daughter for treatment. Rachel was treated with Rock Rose with a Sweet Chestnut supplement, and her condition improved dramatically after two weeks of treatment. She recovered from her state of depression, rediscovered her enthusiasm and realized that there were plenty more fish in the sea. Just four weeks after Bach flower treatment, Rachel began to go out with a new guy; she discarded the feelings of helplessness that had beset her a few weeks previously, and prepared herself for the exciting adventures that life had in store for her.

Extract 6

Cherry Plum

White

Aims to change: a feeling of loss of mental and general control, cruelty, fear of harming oneself and others.

Improves: peace and calm, control over stressful situations and mental stress.

An Overpowering Personality

Bruce was an outstanding personality, dominating any social circle. He had original and creative viewpoints and ideas, and was a strikingly handsome man. He was a dedicated non-conformist, and combined the temperament of an artist with the instincts of a politician. He was a natural-born leader, and his ability to sway others always made him the center of attention. He was highly critical, and was fully aware of his powers of persuasion and of the fact that he could convince others to do illegal or immoral things, or to go against the grain, merely by virtue of his strong personality, abilities, and multifarious talents.

However, Bruce frequently fell victim to anxiety attacks caused by the feeling that he really was leading others astray. Occasionally, he suffered fits of rage, and behaved violently toward others. The straw that broke the camel's back was the day he lost control, and, without premeditation, physically abused his wife. Full of remorse, he did not know how to make amends for what he had done. He writhed in internal agony and ate himself up. He reached a situation where the emotional burden was too heavy for him to bear.

As he had no idea how to cope, he decided to seek

help. He underwent treatment with a Bach flower remedy - Cherry Plum extract - over a period of six weeks, and began feeling a marked improvement in his ability to dominate his uncontrolled impulses. He felt more emotionally relaxed. He overcame his fear of causing harm to people over whom he exerted such a great influence, and learned to neutralize the effect he had on them. Before long he was able to channel his natural talents in a more positive and desirable direction over which he had full control.

Momentary Loss of Control

Natalie lost her husband in a traffic accident, and was now the sole breadwinner for herself and her three small daughters. She was grieved by her husband's death, but worse still was the heavy spiritual and emotional burden of facing life on her own and raising her three little girls alone. Her parents lived far away, and her late husband's parents were too old to be of any assistance.

While her husband was alive, the couple coped with raising their children together without undue difficulty. They helped each other, and cooperated wonderfully. But now, she was desperate with worry about the future, and she often felt she was going to lose her mind with anxiety. There were days when she felt powerless to cope with life's daily worries. She tried her best to cater to all her children's needs and wishes, but sometimes impossible situations cropped up, and she felt she could not go on. When this happened, she would lose total control, and often let off steam by smashing household items. After venting, she would feel some relief from her anger, but then she would burst into bitter tears, and howl like a small child.

Natalie knew that if she did not get help, she would soon be on a short, one-way trip - downward. She was treated with Cherry Plum extract and immediately felt an improvement. Every time she used the remedy she felt herself becoming stronger and, after two months, felt like a new woman. She could function fully, and regained complete control over her life. There were no more emotional outbursts, and Natalie's new-found relaxed attitude undoubtedly gave her the strength she needed to carry on living.

Extracts for the Treatment of Insecurity

Extract 28*

Scleranthus

Green

Aims to change: insecurity, inability to choose between different options.
Improves: peace of mind, decisiveness, the ability to maintain balance, speed of decision and action.

Don't Know, Not Sure
When Rhona found it impossible to make up her mind about a career, she finally reached the breaking-point, and decided to consult with a Bach flower remedy practitioner.

Her inability to decide what was best for her had been a lifelong liability. She had always followed the herd - at school, in the girl scouts - generally waiting to see what her friends were doing and then following suit. She had never stopped to ask herself if that was what she really wanted to do. The main thing for her was to go with the flow and to be like everyone else.

She never stood out in company or expressed her opinions in public. Her insecurity and the fact that she never tried to be herself were expressed in daily matters, such as her taste in clothes, places of entertainment, and so on. She even adopted her parents' political views wholesale, and it did not occur to her to disagree. You could say that she did not have any control over her own life - rather, that life's events and whichever framework she happened to be in at the time influenced her and dictated the way she lived.

Rhona became aware of her spinelessness when she was faced with having to make decisions that would affect the course of the rest of her life. She was confused when she had to make a career choice, and this came to a head when she had no idea in which direction to go. She wanted to receive professional training, but did not know what suited her, or what she was good at, since she had spent her life avoiding thinking about what interested her, and had always followed others.

She knew she had to hone her own individualism and to take heed of her desires and inner feelings if she wanted to change. But it was too difficult a task for her, and she felt that she was losing her bearings. She steadfastly refused to entertain the idea of psychological treatment because deep in her heart she felt that she would find her way on her own.

Eventually, Rhona turned to Bach flower remedies and was treated with Scleranthus for eight weeks. She gradually began to attain equilibrium and peace of mind that gave her a sense of being sure that her decisions were correct for her and appropriate to her talents. For the first time in her life, she actually took stock of herself and thought about what she really wanted, what she was capable of, what she liked, and what she was suited to. She began an inner voyage of self-discovery and relied on her powers of judgment. Ultimately, she succeeded in making crucial decisions regarding the future pattern of her life without the accompanying sense of insecurity. Now she was ready to live an independent life.

Starting Afresh

Every time 17-year-old Stan expressed his political views in public, his friends burst out laughing. In fact, whenever Stan expressed an opinion on any subject, his friends knew that he was just repeating arguments and ideas and reciting speeches he had heard before. His friends would make fun of him, knowing that he would just go along spinelessly with whatever everyone else thought, changing his mind according to the predominant opinion. For his part, Stan was easily convinced by whatever argument was prevalent at the time. He felt that were always two sides to any coin, and every interpretation sounded perfectly acceptable to him.

His friends' laughs and guffaws made Stan feel terribly frustrated, and each time it happened, he felt as if he wanted the earth to swallow him up rather than be exposed to scorn and ridicule. However, he did not know how to put an end to it. Whenever he opened his mouth, he heard laughter at his expense, and when he kept quiet, he was encouraged to voice his "opinion," only to be ridiculed. It was a vicious circle. He was simply incapable of taking a stand, and he often found himself in embarrassing situations in all walks of life. He felt increasingly insecure.

Stan's mother was pained by her son's anguish, his lack of self-confidence, and how it impinged on every aspect of his life. Powerless to endow him with more confidence or relieve his predicament, despite her best efforts, she eventually decided to take Stan for treatment with Bach flower remedies. Stan was treated with Scleranthus for seven weeks. Initially, Stan was more relaxed and calm, and his anxiety level dropped. Then his self-confidence began to improve gradually, and, after a while, he felt he could start afresh. He began to make decisions, follow his own heart, and accomplish the tasks he set himself. His belief in himself increased, as did his self-confidence.

Within a few months, Stan sensed that the people around him had begun to relate to him differently, and the positive feedback he received reinforced him greatly. He suddenly felt that he was in control of his life, and that things were good for him again

Extract 36

Wild Oat

Dark Green

Aims to change: dissatisfaction, ambition without confidence, hesitancy, feeling of not belonging.

Improves: getting ambitions and aspirations in order, knowing one's way in life.

The Prettiest Girl in the Kindergarten

As soon as Diana was born, everyone said that she was going to be the prettiest little girl in the kindergarten. And so it was; she was the queen of the kindergarten, and then of her class, and later grew up to be a gorgeous young woman. As a result of her beauty, she was always the center of attention and was always noticed - whether she wanted to be or not.

Sometimes, her good looks were a disadvantage. She found it hard to make friends with other girls, as they were keenly jealous of her appearance. In an era of myriad soap operas, drama series and multi-channel TV, all featuring stunning actresses with perfect figures, Diana's less blessed friends became increasingly disenchanted with her when they realized that with her looks she could replace any of their TV heroines. Diana was not a brilliant student, but she worked hard and did well.

With her vital statistics - her good high-school graduation grades and her supermodel looks - Diana decided to go out and conquer the world. She had always felt she was worldly-wise, and was sure that she would have no problem eventually attaining a senior position in the State Department, where her sights were set on a high-profile position. She was accepted for a degree in

International Relations and Political Science at college, and in parallel began to work as an airline stewardess.

After completing her studies, and quitting her job at the airline, she applied for an apprentice position at the State Department, and was horrified when her application was rejected. She was not to be deterred, and decided to apply for any position at the ministry with a view to climbing the career ladder once she got in. She was absolutely convinced that she would land a job there, but it was not so easy and, ultimately, she had to exploit her father's connections with someone inside the ministry to get a job.

She started out as assistant manager of the director-general's office. Two years later, she was still in the same job and hated her work. Still, she was dead set on achieving her goal. Three more years went by and nothing changed. By the sixth year, Diana's well-being began to diminish. She felt she was doing a very good job, despite her lack of interest in the work. She also felt that she was over-qualified for the position, and was amazed that the ministry heads had not yet "discovered" her. How could they not have noticed her talent - let alone her looks?

Burnout began to take its toll. The passing years did not help, either. She began to lose her sparkle and was no longer quite the slender, glowing beauty she had always been. She felt stuck, and that she had hit rock bottom - both physically and professionally. Diana, for whom greatness and glory had been predicted, had become a nondescript clerk in a dull government ministry. She began to lose her self-confidence, and her emotional health began to suffer. The fact that she was still unmarried, and no longer in the first flush of youth, only exacerbated her situation. She felt that the promising young girl she had been had disappeared, and that she had missed the opportunity that nature had given her.

Over the years, her mother and sisters had tried to tell her that her aspirations did not exactly tally with her natural abilities, and that perhaps she should think about another, more suitable, line of work. But Diana stuck to her guns, sure that she would hit the jackpot one day, and refused to see the reality of her deteriorating situation. Gradually, she began to realize that she was not going to win the Miss World beauty contest, nor was she going to be appointed Ambassador. She sank into bitter gloom, became agitated and unpleasant, and began to feel that she had missed out on "real" life; she had not even come close to it.

A good friend referred her to treatment with Bach flower remedies, and Diana starting taking Wild Oat extract. She soon began to attain a sense of equilibrium, and was able to compare the expectations she had nurtured with the goals she could realistically hope to achieve. Slowly, she began to get a more balanced picture of the world. She was now capable of setting herself realistic, attainable targets that were more compatible with her natural abilities. She started a job at a public relations company, albeit at a relatively late stage of life, but she felt she could make the most of her abilities there. To her great joy, her bosses noticed her good work, and she received the feedback she needed. Today, Diana has regained her self-confidence and feels she is living a full life.

How Could They Do That to Him?

Jerry was a Capricorn, an incorrigibly ambitious perfectionist. He was dedicated to his work at one of the country's leading telecommunication companies, always working the maximum amount of overtime, and inevitably the last one to go home in the evening. He was not the brightest employee and, in order to be considered one of the best workers in the company, he had to check everything he did. Before submitting a report to his superiors, he would check it two or three times to ensure it was perfect. His seniors, who were aware of his diligence, always praised him, and he hoped he would be the first in line for promotion when the fateful day arrived. In fact, he could not even imagine any other possibility, so he was totally stunned when one of his colleagues got the promotion instead of him.

He went around eating himself up for days on end. Frustrated and bitter, he could not believe that his seniors had seen fit to promote someone else - worse still, a rival of his whom he had seen taking shortcuts and cutting corners, and who was nowhere near as devoted to his work as he was. Nobody was. He was consumed with anger, although outwardly he had to maintain his composure and act as if everything was normal. Inwardly, he felt powerless. He began to feel his strength draining away, and his ambitious drive disappeared. He acted normally, but realized that he could not keep up the act for much longer. He felt cheated and considered leaving the company.

A good friend, who understood how Jerry felt, had a chat with him one evening, calmed him down, and helped him to put things in proportion. He suggested that Jerry try a Bach flower remedy. Jerry underwent treatment with a combination of Wild Oat and Willow extract, and right from the start began feeling that he was regaining his composure. The sense of frustration, anger and dissatisfaction gave way to a better inner feeling, a more balanced view of life, and greater self-awareness. After two weeks of treatment, Jerry felt better at work, and more self-confident. He rediscovered his motivation to succeed, and less than a year later, he received his coveted promotion. Today he is manager of a large department in the company, proud of his success and satisfied with his salary and his status.

Extract 17

Hornbeam

Green

Aims to change: a tendency to procrastinate, although commitments are honored.

Improves: confidence in one's ability to solve problems; issues are handled without delay.

The Happy Wife

Julie was the eldest of three sisters. Her family was wealthy and her parents spoilt her. She never lacked for anything. She was young and talented, and everything came easily to her. She was a good student at school, displaying creativity and originality. She enjoyed social success and popularity among her friends. At college, Julie was a straight-A student in the Biology department, enjoyed a full social life, and, after completing her degree, went into research. She later married a highly intelligent young man, but he was neither very adventurous nor very outgoing.

After eight years of marriage, Julie lost interest in her husband, who no longer added any spice to her life. By now, she was the mother of three young children, and felt trapped. She wanted to do special, different things. She was full of *joie de vivre* and had a lively temperament, but as a result of living with her conservative husband, these attributes had wilted and died. She felt suffocated. On the one hand, her marriage was comfortable and relaxed and provided a safe basis for her life, but she was bored to tears. Julie deliberated long and hard about possibly breaking up the marriage. A divorce would undoubtedly have a bad effect on her children. On the other hand, she felt that if she remained in her marriage, she would dry up and lose her zest for life entirely. She went through a period of internal agonizing without anyone noticing.

She began to lose her natural sparkle. Outwardly, she was forced to act the "happy wife" who wanted for nothing, but inside she was dying. Her energies began draining away and she starting feeling lethargic. She was suffering from emotional exhaustion which threatened to paralyze her. She lost her enthusiasm and vitality, and everything seemed too much for her. She, who had never had to initiate anything because everything always seemed to work out so conveniently for her, was faced with making fateful and significant decisions. She found herself in a situation whereby if she did not take the initiative, nothing would change.

Julie felt confused and muddled, and her inability to figure out what was best for her and how to improve her life threw her into despair. She became depressed and felt as if she were trapped in a snowball that was speeding out of control and growing all the time.

Her closest friend came to her rescue. She was the only person in whom Julie confided. The friend had had an amazing and welcome experience with Bach flower remedies, and she persuaded Julie to undergo treatment with them.

Julie was treated with a Hornbeam remedy over a period of several weeks. The effect was immediate, and she felt she was regaining her self-confidence. She felt able to take responsibility for her own life and to change her approach. Suddenly, she could make decisions, accomplish all her previous irksome daily chores and tasks with ease, and honor the commitments she had taken upon herself. Gradually, the feeling of tiredness and powerlessness dissipated, and she changed the way she lived to suit her life as it is today. The treatment helped her to preserve the life she had built for herself without sacrificing her children or her husband. She now lives life to the full, and is the happy mother of four children, after deciding to have another child of her own free will and as an expression of love.

Her Fall and Rise

Mary was a well-known actress in one of the country's leading theater companies. She had become a household name after appearing in a string of successful shows. However, her star starting falling after a number of plays in which she appeared flopped. Her career took a nose-dive and her halcyon days appeared to be over. Mary found it hard to accept that the good times were gone, and that she was passed her prime. Approaching old age also began to leave its mark on her and, after becoming apathetic about her predicament, she began to put on weight. Mary, who until fairly recently had been pestered by playwrights and inundated with requests to play leading roles, had to start auditioning in an attempt to win a part.

As the years went by, the number of beautiful young actresses with whom she had to compete for parts increased, and she became desperate. People in the street no longer recognized her. Life did not shine upon her any more, and she could not countenance making a career change. Mary began to lose interest in life. She did not care what became of her; she became apathetic and disinterested, and it looked like she had lost her will to live. She had no idea how to extricate herself from her situation and take herself in hand. At times, it was so bad that she felt like the "living dead." The woman who had been at the hub of the city's social life, active and involved in politics - to the point that she could express her opinion whenever she liked and feel that she had the power to change things - was now completely indifferent. Nothing interested her anymore. All she waited for was the "miracle" that would get her out of the mess she was in.

Mary looked ghastly. Her condition deteriorated to such an extent that she felt embarrassed to leave the house in case someone recognized her, and her pathetic state became grist for the gossip columnists' mill. She knew that, somehow, she had to break the vicious circle if she wanted to improve her lot.

Salvation came in the form of a Bach flower remedy. When Mary started treatment with Hornbeam, she was despondent, tired, listless and apathetic. Gradually, this feeling started to disappear, and Mary felt her energies flooding back to her. Her emotional recovery began. She started to feel a sense of renewal and caring, and began to take care of her appearance. She lost weight and looked a lot better. She felt she was returning to the land of the living and rediscovered her zest both for her professional life and for things going on around her.

Six months later, Mary returned to the stage and landed a major part in a successful show put on by the theater in which she had previously starred. Her return to cultural life marked the beginning of a new era for her, and she is eternally grateful for having taken the Bach remedy that got her back on track.

Extract 5

Cerato*

Blue

Aims to change: doubting one's own powers of judgment, dependence on advice and approval, often following incorrect advice.

Improves: provides gentle support and approval, the ability to intuitively choose a correct line of action or advice.

Lacking Moral Fiber

Ralph was an indecisive character who was capable of changing his mind practically every time the wind changed direction. He was so lacking in confidence that he would examine any decision he had made from every possible angle, finding numerous shortcomings and eventually concluding that it was a bad decision in the first place. His lack of confidence repeatedly undermined any stand he took or opinion he formed.

The most serious symptom of this was not his inability to adhere to his decisions or stick to his guns, but the deterioration in his interpersonal relations. Not only was he considered to be completely spineless, but his insecurity would prompt him to ask others for advice about even the most minor of mundane matters. Things became so bad that he would constantly bother people for advice. He found himself in embarrassing situations. People began to mock him and to deride him for being unable to stick to his guns, and for his never-ending need to clarify his position vis-à-vis his surroundings. In a desperate attempt to avoid being laughed at, Ralph became the laughing-stock of his colleagues, immediate and distant alike. Their insults cut him to the quick, and he was anything but immune to them. Quite the contrary, Ralph was a sensitive person who was extremely aware of his predicament.

Fortunately, this very awareness and sensitivity led Ralph - not before undergoing a protracted period of deliberation during which he changed his mind a thousand times - to opt for Bach treatment. A close friend, who knew what he was going through and had witnessed his hesitations, spoke to him frankly. Eventually, he went for treatment.

He was treated with Cerato over a period of three weeks. The improvement was palpable from the very first week. He felt an astonishing improvement in his self-confidence. His ability to make, stick to, and implement decisions soared, and he began to "connect" with his inner thoughts and desires. He was now able to make decisions about what was good for him, and what he should ignore. He became sure of his opinions, presented his views confidently, and stuck to his guns. Ralph underwent a metamorphosis, became self-assured, and developed the capacity to handle the everyday occurrences that constitute life.

An End to Suffering

Gary lost his father as a child, and the loss may have been the reason why Gary stuttered so badly. Be that as it may, Gary grew up with a heavy stammer, getting stuck on every second word. Sometimes he gave up trying to express an opinion or to participate in a conversation, so as not to draw attention to himself and his stammer. Children are a cruel breed, and his childhood was a continuous litany of humiliation and insults. His self-confidence diminished as he grew up, and more than once he adopted the opinions of others just to appease them and to make himself socially acceptable. However, whenever his mother suggested that he be treated for his stammer and cured of it, Gary objected. He was sure that one day he would overcome the problem on his own. He seemed to be in a state of denial, preferring to cherish the illusion that his stammer was a minor issue that could be overcome, if he so wished.

When Gary reached adolescence, and his friends starting dating girls, his stammer become even worse, and he lost the last vestiges of his self-confidence. He was also convinced that he was extremely ugly with his acne, and there were days when he wanted the earth to swallow him up, rather than leave the house to go to school.

Gary's mother decided that it was high time to put an end to her son's suffering by taking to him to a special class for people who stuttered. This time she was determined to solve the problem.

But before she raised the issue, she decided to take him to a Bach flower remedy practitioner so that Gary himself could reach the conclusion that he needed treatment to get rid of the stammer. Gary started taking Cerato extract and, over a four-week period, he began to feel that his approach to life was changing. Everything suddenly took on different proportions. The level of stress at which he lived dropped, and he felt more relaxed with himself and those around him. The extract enabled Gary to regain his self-confidence, and his new-found peace of mind enabled him to tackle his difficulties with a strength and an intensity he had never known previously.

Extract 12*

Gentian

Purple/Lilac

Aims to change: giving up easily and quickly, weakness of character, despondency, and falling into depression easily.

Improves: optimism, not being influenced by past events, steadfastness, single-mindedness.

The Light At The End of the Tunnel

Tessa's husband had left her for another woman, obliging her to raise her son on her own. She was 33 years old at the time - the age at which many woman have reached a stage when the family is beginning to become more financially stable, and the mother can begin to focus more on herself. Since her husband left, Tessa felt she was losing control; this was manifested in all areas of her life. She started to lose interest in her work, and was easily distracted. Her thoughts wandered aimlessly, and she often found herself staring into space for a long time. Day-to-day survival, as well as looking after her son on her own, was very difficult for her, and her physical and spiritual energies began to wane. Increasingly frequently, she slept all afternoon while her seven-year-old son watched TV or played with the computer or with the neighbor's son. Tessa started neglecting herself and putting on weight. She had always looked after her figure, but now she put on over 20 pounds and stopped her weekly visits to the beauty parlor.

She withdrew into herself more and more, although she did not allow herself to sink into a total depression, as she had to look after her son. Because of him, she was forced to function and stay in touch with reality. She felt that her energies had drained away, and that she did not have the strength to cope with reality. But, after a year of almost total detachment from the life she had led previously, she realized that she had to take herself in hand, otherwise her son would suffer. She underwent Bach flower treatment and, initially, took rescue remedy (a blend of five different Bach remedies used for emergencies) and Gentian. The treatment altered her feeling of utter failure and of inability to cope with reality. She began to feel her strength returning and regained her optimism about the future. There was, after all, a light at the end of the tunnel.

The trauma she had experienced began to recede into the past, and she started to pull herself out of her depression. At first, she began to go out to meet with friends she had not seen for a long time. As a result of these outings, she began to take care of her figure and appearance again. Her spirits rose as her appearance improved, and her performance at work picked up. All this had a positive effect on her relationship with her son. The more she devoted herself to him, the better she felt; she was more at one with herself, and gained a greater degree of peace of mind. The road to full recovery was clear, and within a year she embarked on a relationship with a man - something that would have been unthinkable just 12 months earlier.

Snail Woman
Eileen was born with a silver spoon in her mouth. She grew up in a fancy house in one of the wealthiest areas of town, and she had everything she needed or wanted in material terms. Because of the upper-middle-class neighborhood in which she lived, she had to compete with a lot of bright and successful children at primary school, and competition was fierce. It was sometimes overt, sometimes hidden - but there was always a feeling of "I'm smarter / brighter / better than you" in the air.

Although Eileen was not among the weaker students - she was above average - she felt that she was a failure and that she lagged behind the top students. This irked her greatly. Whenever she felt like that, all she wanted to do was curl up like a snail and hide away in her shell, so that no one would notice her. It is likely that her fear of failure stemmed from her home. Both her parents were college professors, and her older brothers were straight-A students at the most prestigious schools in town.

When Eileen grew up and set out on her own, she was constantly bothered by a sense of inadequacy, that she was the weak link in the family. Whenever she undertook a task, she planned it from A to Z so as to avoid any chance of failure and to ensure complete success. Sometimes it worked, and sometimes it didn't. When the latter happened, she felt so completely worthless and despairing that she would fall into a real depression. She immediately stopped believing in herself and her abilities, and was caught up in a vicious circle. Every time she found herself in this non-coping situation, she would throw in the towel and give up without a fight.

After Eileen got married, her married life went from one crisis to the next. Her husband, with the best will in the world to help and understand her, also reached breaking-point. He decided she needed help and persuaded her to try treatment with Bach flower remedies.

Eileen was treated with Gentian, and her self-doubt began to diminish. Her fits of severe depression vanished, her general spiritual well-being improved, and she found it increasingly easier to cope with difficult situations. The problems she had previously found insurmountable now seemed manageable. She felt that if she mustered her strength and used all her natural abilities, she could handle almost any problem. She was able to look back and laugh at the things she had previously found impossible to cope with. She now viewed life from the correct perspective and adopted a positive and optimistic philosophy. In her case, her husband's support was considerable and significant. By the end of her treatment, Eileen had almost entirely rid herself of her tendency to sink into depression and a sense of failure every time something went wrong and not exactly according to plan. Not only did her life change unrecognizably, her entire family reaped the benefits of her recovery.

Extract 13

Gorse

Yellow

Aims to change: despair and extreme hopelessness, pessimism, a negative attitude, the sense of "what's the use..."

Improves: positive faith, hope, belief in one's ability to overcome problems.

Missing Mom

Dana's mother died in a car accident when Dana was 15. The tragedy of her mother's death occurred when Dana was at a confused stage of her development anyway - an adolescent at the age of self-discovery. She was prone to extreme mood-swings: She could look in the mirror one moment and feel like a bombshell, and a moment later she might discover a zit and her self-confidence would plummet. She was at an age when sex and its joys were becoming important. She was only interested in dating boys, knowing who was going with whom, and having a good time at parties and with friends. She began to neglect her studies. When the tragedy occurred, it cut short her youth in one fell swoop. Dana had been very close to her mother. Unlike other teenage girls, Dana told her mother all her most intimate secrets. Dana's mother had been her best friend, and now she she was no longer around.

Dana found it very difficult to adjust. Her two younger brothers adapted more quickly. Dana withdrew into herself and, instead of the merry, boisterous girl she had been before, full of life and joy, Dana became closed and quiet, and hardly went out. She never suggested going out with her friends, and only left the house to attend school or when it was absolutely necessary.

Instead of time helping to heal the wound, Dana's state continued to deteriorate, and she felt there was no point in living. Nothing had any value, and any effort she made seemed a pointless waste of time. "What's the use?" became an expression that Dana often used.

Her pessimism encroached on every area of her life. She could not imagine a brighter future because, anyway, her mother would not be there to share her joys and experiences with her or hear her stories. In addition, the sense that death was so close to her made her view life as unimportant. Why make an effort if she was going to die in the end anyway? Death was lurking in every corner. She felt that even if she went out in the morning, there was no guarantee that she would return home in the evening.

Dana's father, who was initially wrapped up in his own grief, failed to notice the change that had come over his daughter. But now he started to realize that while the other members of the family had started to pick up the pieces and get back to normal, Dana was nowhere near that stage.

He tried to encourage her and talk to her. He tried to get her to seek psychological help. But nothing helped; Dana refused to be comforted. A year after the tragedy, Dana's father decided to send her to a Bach flower practitioner for treatment. To his great surprise, she agreed.

Initially, she was treated with Gorse extract and a number of other extracts, including Gentian. The sense of despair and pessimism she had felt for a whole year began to be replaced by a feeling of optimism, and Dana began to believe she could extricate herself from her crisis and get on with her life. For the first time, she thought it might be possible to manage without her mother, and she began to regain her energy and independence. She started taking an interest in the world around her, and gradually began to go out to meet friends and have a good time. She still suffered from episodes of despondency, when everything looked black, but she could now see the way out of these dark tunnels. She knew she could view life more positively and get back into the thick of things, like before.

Perfectionist

Ruth was a Linguistics professor at a college. She was 56 years old and unmarried. She had never been married, and knew that her chances of finding a partner at her age were slim. She reckoned there were three reasons why she had never married: her domineering father, who had caused her to fear men, her oppressive childhood in a small village, and her own ascetic character that any normal man would find hard to live with. She would not compromise. In retrospect, she felt it had been a mistake not to give any man a fighting chance at being her life true partner, but she knew that now it was too late.

Ruth was not easy to get along with, and she demanded the same level of perfection from those around her as she expected of herself. As a result of her intellectual integrity and her exaggerated need to excel in everything she did, she found herself becoming increasingly despondent. She had suffered from depression all her life, and she waged a constant battle to fend off her feelings of despair. Her condition had become more severe in recent years. Her depressions, which had once been sporadic, became more frequent and, other than going out to lecture at the college, she would spend entire days in bed.

She knew there was no savior waiting around the corner, and that she had to cope with the situation and extricate herself from it - the sooner the better. There was no one close to her to encourage her to snap out of it, so she never allowed herself to sink so low that she lost touch with reality.

She started taking a Bach flower remedy - first Gorse and then Hornbeam - and the effect was almost instantaneous. She found it easier to get out of bed in the morning and start the new day. The world seemed a brighter place, and she began to care about herself and her appearance. To her amazement, she was suffused with a sense of optimism and a feeling that that "everything will turn out OK." She began to be more active socially, and her social circle broadened. She became aware, once again, that the title of Doctor impressed many people. The fact that she had achieved something significant in her life contributed to her pride in herself and her acknowledgment of her own value.

Her whole approach to the world changed and she rediscovered her purpose in life and her reasons for living.

Extracts for the Treatment of Apathy (Detachment from Reality)

Extract 37

Wild Rose

Pink, Red, Yellow

Aims to change: submissiveness, apathy, lack of resistance, lack of ambition and drive.
Improves: vitality, interest in everything.

Barbie Doll

Denise was a refined woman, with a "Barbie doll" appearance.

She kept up with the latest fashions and was meticulous about the way she dressed and put on her make-up. Everything was color-coordinated - her lipstick and her dress, her bag and her shoes, and so on - and her clothes closet was full of mini-dresses, high leather boots, fur coats and the like.

She was absolutely terrified of cockroaches. The sight of a cockroach was enough to provoke hysterical screaming, and her neighbors knew they would have no peace and quiet until someone came to get rid of the offensive creature. She had never been stung by a bee, as she would make herself scarce as soon as she saw one.

One day, she went with a friend to the beach. She did

not like going into the water, and she was one of those "belles" who adorn the beach in velvet swimsuits that serve a decorative purpose only. The two women found a spot near some flowering bushes with marvelously scented blossoms. While they were sunbathing, Denise stretched out her hand to get a pack of cigarettes from her bag. She felt a sudden deep sharp prick and immediately knew a bee had stung her because she had seen one nearby only a few moments earlier. She emitted a tremendous scream: The very person who had always been so careful to steer clear of the "pests" had fallen victim to one. Her screams got even louder when she saw the sting protruding from her skin, and the bee lying dead on her towel. Of course, everyone on the beach gathered round to see what calamity had befallen her. One man removed the sting, and another ran to the nearby kiosk to bring some ice cubes. But nothing could calm her down; Denise was hysterical, panic-stricken and in shock.

Fortunately, there was another woman about her age on the beach who practiced Bach flower treatment and who lived nearby. She ran home and came back with a Wild Rose extract and rubbed some drops into the place where Denise had been stung. Denise calmed down immediately. Her fears and feeling of panic disappeared, and she recovered from her shock sufficiently to be able to pull herself together and go home.

Since that incident, Denise takes a bottle of Wild Rose extract with her everywhere - just in case. No bee will ever throw her into a state of shock and lack of control again.

Inheriting Dad's Business

Chris was 35 years old, married and father of two, when the idea of starting his own business began to take root. He had all the necessary skills. He had studied Business Management in college, and his father ran an industrial oil importing company. If he wanted, Chris could join the firm and take over after his father's retirement.

Chris had never had to work too hard to earn a living.

His parents had made life easy for him during his student days by financing his studies and paying the rent. They even provided him with generous pocket money so that he could devote himself to his studies without having to waste time doing some "menial" job like security work or waiting on tables, like most of his fellow students did.

When he got married, his parents bought the young couple an apartment. His father even pulled strings for Chris to get a job in a prestigious company. Chris had never had any particular need to exert himself, and he began to get bored with life. Nothing was motivating him to get ahead, he had no incentive to make an effort, and he had no coveted goals to aim for.

When Chris decided to leave his job and start working with his father, there was a proviso: His father would take him into the company on condition that he first set up his own small business and prove he was capable of running a company with everything that entails - pressures, perseverance, and so on. Chris, who had never initiated anything, and was not an entrepreneur by nature, was very disappointed. He knew that this was a real test, and was convinced that he would not be able to make a success of it. He almost gave up before he started. He knew he had never aspired to obtain anything more than he already had because he had enough, but he very much wanted to change his life.

The situation was resolved by two considerations: First, the monotony of his life, which lacked the slightest bit of excitement; everything was routine, predictable, and frustratingly boring. Second, his wife knew that her husband had good managerial abilities, despite his lack of vision and creativity, and that he would do a first-class job if he took over his father's business.

Chris underwent treatment with Bach flower remedies in order to overcome the anxiety he felt at the thought of establishing his own business, and in order to boost his confidence in his ability to take the initiative and undertake such a project. He was treated with Wild Rose and soon felt an inner enthusiasm that generated great excitement about the project that lay ahead of him. He began to believe in his own abilities and in the possibility of realizing his full potential.

In the end, Chris coped successfully with the new project. He had shaken off his state of total stagnation, mainly as a result of his new, deep-rooted faith in himself.

Extract 35

White Chestnut

Yellow/Red

Aims to change: anxious and undesirable thoughts, stubbornness, mental conflict.

Improves: peace of mind, tranquillity, not bothered by outside influences.

Warm Family Man

Geoffrey was a warm family man who loved his wife and two small children very much. But his involvement with his family life had become obsessive. Matters deteriorated to the extent that getting up in the morning to go to work became nightmarish. He would get up early to go to the children's beds and wake them, kiss them and inhale their warm scent. He would call them "hot cakes." After the regular ritual of cuddling each child in their bed, he would leave their room, go through his normal routine of dressing in his neatly pressed suit and tie, and leave for work.

As soon as he had managed to navigate his way through the traffic to work and had sat down at his desk, he would call his wife, who worked near their home, to ask her how the morning had gone with the kids - how she had left them at kindergarten or school, what each one had said, and if either of them had had a hard time saying goodbye to her. He was not deterred by the fact that his wife's response was always identical, and he kept up his daily habit of calling her as soon as he reached the office. Geoffrey would call his wife every hour or two to make sure that everything was all right. Sometimes she would laugh at him and inquire whether he had enough work to do, because he seemed to have so much free time to spend on the phone. He wanted to know when she had picked up the kids, what they had eaten, where and how they were spending their afternoon, and so on. Every detail interested him, and he had to feel he was in touch with what was happening at home, even in his absence. Geoffrey was considered a good worker - efficient and creative - but his colleagues laughed at his peculiar behavior behind his back, and scoffed at his obsession with having to know what was happening with his family on a minute-to-minute basis. Although Geoffrey realized that he was different in this respect, he merely thought he was a better family man than most.

Geoffrey's wife was the main victim of his behavior. She often complained about it to him, and could not understand why he was so obsessed with everything to do with his family, or where the obsession stemmed from. She had never been unfaithful to him and loved him very much, and she knew that he knew this, so she was sure that this was not the reason for his anxiety. She tried a subtle approach to get him to change and, when she saw that this was to no avail, she adopted a more direct approach. But nothing helped. She felt as if she was a fugitive, under constant surveillance. Even when she went out with the children, she always took her cell-phone with her so that her husband would be able to contact her. She knew she would have to face the music when she got home if she had been inaccessible for a moment. But when the children started to answer his phone calls with: "Not you again!" Geoffrey realized he needed to change his ways.

Whenever he was at work and felt the urge to call home, he would fight the temptation and postpone it for a while. But five minutes later, his hand would reach out for the phone and he would call again. He knew he had to resort to a more drastic course of action.

He turned to Bach flower treatment for help and was treated with White Chestnut extract; it had an immediate effect on him. He became more relaxed, and even his physical movements became more fluid and less agitated. The peace of mind he had achieved allowed him to view life more objectively, and he was now able to look at himself from a distance. Suddenly, his abnormal behavior came into sharp focus, and more than ever, he could understand that his anxiety over the welfare of his family was exaggerated and unjustified. Once he realized that, far from helping, he was being extremely tiresome, he changed his behavior quickly. He stopped being obsessive about calling home - to the point that he was content to call home only twice a day. His family breathed a sigh of relief, and his productivity increased out of all recognition.

Food Obsession
Gillian was constantly worried about her figure and her weight. She had a tendency to put on weight, and counted every calorie that she swallowed. Her battle with her desire to eat started from the moment she woke up in the morning.

If she could have permitted herself, she would have begun the day with a couple of hot bagels, butter, smoked salmon and cream cheese. Later she would have a healthy sandwich for her mid-morning break, a calorie-rich lunch with a creamy dessert, followed by cake and ice cream at five o'clock, and a dairy meal consisting of a tasty quiche, pasta or a fancy salad with a thick, calorie-rich dressing in the evening. But all this was a fantasy.

In reality, she would start the day with a diet cracker, followed by cooked vegetables and lean meat for lunch; she permitted herself the "luxury" of a yogurt with cereal in the evening. This regimen enabled her to have a slim figure and, although she was pleased with her slender body, she was prone to frequent lapses when she would binge. Naturally, she would put on weight - and would then return to her strict diet. This was basically the routine of her life.

More than anything else, Gillian wanted to free herself of this obsession and her unceasing involvement with food. She could not stop thinking about what she was going to have for lunch, and how many calories there were in a particular meal. If she "cheated" during the morning, or ate a bit of cake, she would "sentence" herself to fasting from the evening until the following morning. She thought about food the whole time, and her only consolation was her slim body, of which she was very proud.

While she knew that she did not fit the medical profile of an anorexic, she was displaying similar symptoms, and wanted to rid herself of her obsession with food and her figure. She started taking White Chestnut extract, and the effect was almost immediate. Her obsession with food began to diminish, and she noticed that other things were becoming more important to her, such as the day-to-day hassles of her job. She felt she was overcoming her chronic condition, and discovered that there was a whole world out there, with numerous fields of interest for her. Her narrow world expanded, and her perspective changed to the point that even if she put on a few extra pounds, it was not the end of the world.

She felt that she had finally attained some kind of equilibrium between her physical and psychological conditions.

Extract 9*

Clematis

Light Blue

Aims to change: daydreaming, inability to concentrate, lethargy, indifference, escaping from reality.

Improves: discovering an interest in everything, inspiration, being artistic and practical.

Doesn't Miss Out On Life Anymore

Alan was a popular and famous songwriter whose songs were frequently played on the radio. His private life, in contrast, was far from successful. His creative drive was so strong that it dominated his life uncontrollably. His urge to create was much stronger than he was.

Alan was unfocused, and often seemed not to be listening when spoken to. It was if he was not entirely there, and occasionally seemed unable to communicate with those around him. He was miles away, and appeared deeply immersed in thought. He had a faraway look in his eyes, which were always half-closed, never fully open. He dressed in a disheveled manner, and adopted the image of the "cool" artist. Alan never revealed his true feelings or displayed real happiness or sorrow. He acted as if he did not care about what was going on around him, although those close to him knew that that was not always the case; his facade, his seeming uninvolvement, could be misleading.

Alan consulted with a Bach flower remedy practitioner after he became concerned about his relationships with women. He had never managed to build a strong, meaningful relationship, and was incapable of showing that he really cared. This caused most of the women he dated to dump him sooner or later. Alan realized that he needed to change his personality and behavior radically if he wanted to build a serious relationship with someone. He understood that there was some basic element in him that deterred women, but, although tried to work on himself, he was unable to make any headway.

Alan was treated with Clematis extract and, as the treatment progressed, he felt that he was more and more in touch with people. He became more caring and aware of the needs of others, and realized that things were no longer passing him by. This inner change gained impetus, and the people around him immediately noticed the difference. The feedback he received was so positive that he wanted to continue to even greater achievements. After a while, when he felt ready, he resolved to win back an ex-girlfriend who had left him when she felt that he was not sufficiently interested in her or in being with her. At first, Alan thought that he would have to fight to get her back. He did not imagine that the change in him was so profound that taking an interest in other people was now second nature to him. The woman had also noticed the enormous change that had come over him, and she gladly resumed their relationship. Eighteen months later they got married, and today they have a son whom Alan adores. Alan still wonders whether he would have been able to reach this happy state had it not been for the revolutionary change in his life.

At the Very Root of Reality

Helen had had a very difficult childhood. Her mother had abused her physically and emotionally, and the resulting scars, particularly the emotional ones, influenced the way she related to the world around her. She kept herself to herself and endeavored to maintain a distance from others so as not to get hurt. She preferred spending her spare time alone; the main thing was not to get into a situation of intimacy with anyone. At work, Helen shared an office with three other women of her age, but despite the intimacy that is a natural consequence of the work situation, especially with women, who tend to share personal confidences about domestic or feminine matters, Helen never revealed her feelings or her secret thoughts to them. She remained aloof. Occasionally she was the butt of the odd snide remark, but Helen never let it affect her behavior. As a graphic artist, her job required creative ability. The nature of the work allowed her to detach herself from her surroundings and devote her full attention to the computer. She hardly talked. Her link with reality and with those around her was very weak. Her main connection to real life occurred with regard to things like checking her bank balance, and paying her rent and other bills on time. Her colleagues called her "spaced out," and she took it as a compliment. She was considered very creative, and her work was highly esteemed, particularly by her employers. Although she worked a bit slowly, and did not always produce exactly what the customer wanted, everyone agreed that all her projects were real works of art.

One day, her employers called her into their office and informed her that they wanted to promote her to team manager. They said, however, that they were not absolutely sure if she would fit the bill, as the new position required management skills, and she would have to prove that she had what it took. What attracted her most was the generous raise in salary that she was to receive with the promotion. Helen decided that she had to get a hold of herself, take responsibility, and show she cared, in order to prove to her bosses that she could do the job.

She consulted with a Bach flower remedy practitioner and was treated with Clematis extract. Her ability to focus on things in which she was not particularly interested improved significantly. For the first time, she began to cooperate with those around her and develop a relationship with her colleagues. This was new to her, and she began to like it. At last she felt she was a part of the world around her, rather than being detached from it. While she had previously felt as if life was passing her by, now she felt that life was passing right through her, and that she was taking an active part in it. Her feet were firmly planted on the ground, and everything interested her - from TV shows that she had never had the slightest interest in watching, to the private lives of her colleagues.

The change was dramatic. After a couple of months, during which her bosses and colleagues noticed her new attitude, she became the talk of the company. She even greeted people whom she had previously ignored with a cheery "Good morning" every day. Some jokingly inquired whether she had a new boyfriend.

Helen got the promotion and displayed satisfactory management skills, which delighted both her and her colleagues.

Honeysuckle

Orange/Coral

Aims to change: nostalgia, living in the past, dwelling on past successes, pleasures and glory.

Improves: learning the lessons of previous experiences while feeling sadness or happiness.

The Bubble

Dave was a product of his environment - the small urban neighborhood in which he had grown up, where most of the locals were academics, intellectuals and media people - the elite, in short. He attended the best primary school in town, followed by the most prestigious high school, where he was an outstanding student. Both his parents were college professors, and he grew up in a narrow, cosseted environment.

His social circle remained constant from kindergarten onward. He knew his peers intimately and he socialized with the same people throughout his childhood and into adulthood. There were few opportunities to mix with other segments of the population. The members of his circle considered themselves superior, poked fun at the less fortunate, and never mixed with people who lived on the "wrong side of the tracks." Dave and his friends related to them like refugees from the Third World, and they thought they would never want, or be able, to communicate with them on the same level. The arrogance that characterized both Dave and his peers ran in their veins.

After graduating from high school, Dave joined the armed forces, and served in an elite unit together with his friends. Once again, Dave was cosseted from the outside world. But all this changed when Dave started feeling dissatisfied with his army service and decided to ask for a transfer to a regular unit. Upon reaching the artillery unit to which he had been assigned, he was appalled by his new comrades-in-arms. Instead of the sparkling, elitist society in which he had spent his entire life, here he met a whole cross-section of society. There were immigrants from all over the world, and he found their manners and speech repugnant. He referred to them privately as "those people," as primitive, stupid, and even bestial. In comparison to them, with his refined background and completely different outlook, he felt like an alien from outer space. He had to get used to something that he felt he could never accept. But he also discovered that he, who had always prided himself on being open-minded and non-racist, held deep-rooted prejudices that he had to eradicate.

He was in total shock about his new surroundings. He kept thinking about the friends he had left behind in the other unit, and sank into deep gloom. He could not stop thinking about his happy childhood and his close-knit circle of friends. On the other hand, he knew that he could not continue living within that protected world, and now he had an opportunity to become acquainted with the "outside world," and get a taste of what was awaiting him later in life. He knew that, whether he wanted to or not, he would one day have to deal with other kinds of people.

His state of depression and shock led him to seek treatment with Bach flower extracts. He was given Honeysuckle that cushioned the shock he had experienced. Gradually, the heavy burden of nostalgia that had enveloped him began to lift. He learned how to detach himself from the influences of his former closed society, and began to become more receptive to the unfamiliar people among whom he now found himself. Something inside him softened, and his previously rigid mindset became more liberal, enabling him to settle down. The Bach flower treatment gradually helped Dave to come to terms with his place in his new surroundings. As time progressed, Dave got to know his fellow soldiers, and discovered that they weren't so bad after all. He actually started to like being with them and found their very different approach to life, the way they thought and spoke, and their openness, intriguing. By the end of his military service, two of his comrades had become his best friends, and they still are to this day. All three are now married and have families, and they all meet up regularly on social occasions.

Breaking Away from Nostalgia

Jeremy was 29 when his girlfriend left him after a six-year relationship. They had planned to get married and had even set a date and a place. Jeremy was deeply in love with his girlfriend; he had never felt such strong feelings for any other woman before. He was certain that this was the love of his life. His girlfriend seemed to feel the same until the day she bumped into an ex-boyfriend - and they resumed their friendship. Meanwhile, things began to go wrong with her relationship with Jeremy, and she decided to go back to her former lover. Jeremy was shattered. He could not believe that the love of his life could do such a thing to him.

At first, he found it hard to function on a day-to-day basis. But he was an emotionally strong person, and he knew he had to swallow his pride, pick up the pieces, and get on with his life. Despite his determination to leave the whole business behind, he was haunted mercilessly by memories of their love, visions of nights of passion they had shared, trips they had taken together, and other happy experiences they had shared.

Because of the long period of time they had spent together, Jeremy found it very hard to get by without his former girlfriend. He was overcome with nostalgia every time he looked at photographs of the two of them, every time he wore clothes they had bought together, and every time he said something she would have said. He was struggling to shake off the past, and felt he needed help to alleviate the process of "mourning."

He began to take Honeysuckle extract, and gradually the scenes from the past, the feelings, the scents and the shared experiences began to fade. He could go through whole days without feeling the bonds of the past, and, as time progressed, he became increasingly freer. Finally, his inner feelings convinced him - not just theoretically - that he was yearning for something that would never return. With the help of the extract, Jeremy succeeded in shaking off memories and thoughts about the past, and he began to function normally again - much better than he ever thought possible.

Extract 7

Chestnut Bud

Green

Aims to change: a tendency to repeat mistakes, not learn the lessons of the past.

Improves: an ability to see things clearly, to learn from previous experiences.

Power Drunk

Cheryl was a simple woman. As a child she had grown up among hard-working, blue-collar people, However, her home environment was warm and supportive, and her parents encouraged her to succeed in life. Although she was not particularly bright, and had not graduated from high school, by the age of 35 Cheryl had attained the position of manager of a large department in one of the country's leading cosmetics companies. She strode around the company with a sense of great pride, and felt that she was in a position of great power. She enjoyed giving orders, acting with authority, and being responsible for the final decisions on a large range of issues. Work was her entire life, and she was intoxicated with the power she had as department manager. Her authority to occasionally make important decisions, like deciding the fate of an employee, had gone to her head.

She was, however, wracked by a constant desire to please others, and often ingratiated herself with the other employees. Sometimes she behaved so obsequiously that the workers laughed at her behind her back. But when she felt she was dropping to their level and becoming too familiar with them, she suddenly worried that they might think of her as "one of them." Then she changed abruptly from being a sweet, pleasant person to an aggressive character who made it clear to them who the boss was. These transitions were very sharp. If she exchanged harsh words with an employee, she would remind the person that he/she worked for her, and not the other way round. The workers used to imitate her during the lunch break, scoffing at some of things she had said to them that day. Despite her desire to be pleasant and a good boss, Cheryl did not know how to set clear boundaries. She did not know where her territory as a boss ended, and the status of friend started, and because she was terrified of jeopardizing her managerial status, she repeatedly made the same mistake by coming out with one of her notorious gems, which, far from making her subordinates respect her, made her the object of their scorn.

Her superior knew that Cheryl had good managerial abilities and that she was basically a good soul. She spoke to her on several occasions, and repeatedly explained the mistakes she was making with the workers. Cheryl promised to mend her ways and understood where she was going wrong. In spite of this, she continued to make the same mistakes, as if her superior had never spoken to her, as if she had not taken any of the remarks on board.

When things got worse, some of the workers began to complain about Cheryl's intolerable attitude toward them, particularly her unpredictable behavior. Cheryl's superior realized that unless Cheryl changed her behavior with the workers, she would have to fire her, despite her good managerial skills. Cheryl's boss called her in for a talk and laid things on the line. Cheryl understood that she would have to make a big effort if she wanted to keep her job.

She started taking Chestnut Bud extract, and this helped her to focus on the smaller things in life. She began to notice things she had never seen before. She finally understood what her boss had been trying to tell her all this time, and what she meant when she spoke about changing her attitude toward her subordinates. Like a drunkard coming out of an alcoholic stupor, she saw things in a different light, and began to understand why her tone of voice, the things she said, and her behavior toward her subordinates were inappropriate to her status. The fine line between being a boss and a friend became clearer.

Suddenly, she realized why her workers had scorned her, and understood their cynical attitude. Her level of consciousness rose and, with it, her entire world began to change. She adopted a different attitude toward her subordinates, and they felt the change in her behavior toward them. They now related to her completely differently. Of course, Cheryl kept her job. The extract helped her put things right - things she had previously had no idea how to handle. For someone for whom work was her whole life, the extract had worked wonders.

The brawnier, the better!

By the age of 40, Elizabeth had managed to marry and get divorced four times. She was basically a conventional "good girl" who only wanted a warm home and a supportive family around her. However, time after time, she found herself with the wrong partner. Every time she got married, she discovered that her husband operated on the wrong side of the law. She had grown up in a strict home, and here she was, attracted to small-time hoods and law-breakers. Despite her conventional appearance, Elizabeth was drawn to adventures and to out-of-the-ordinary and unusual events. The men to whom she was attracted were big, because she liked to feel small and helpless in their company. All her men were muscular types and looked like members of the Mafia. They were not really criminals, however - they just walked the fine line between the law and what was beyond it. They liked to test the limits of social norms.

Time after time, she left her partners because she was unable to communicate with them on the same intellectual level. She always discovered, in the end, that she was brighter than they were, and had more talent, more moral fiber and more integrity. She was always attracted to the same type, even though the end of the relationship was a foregone conclusion. In spite of this, she maintained a cheerful outlook, and repeatedly felt that she had finally found Mr. Right, with whom she would live happily ever after. Every time the relationship fell through, she was mortified, and each time it happened it was harder and more bitter for her. As the years passed, her children by her various husbands became involved in the break-ups.

At the age of 40, after her fourth divorce, she decided that she would not repeat the same mistake. She felt she was still young enough to remarry, but this time she was not going to take any undue risks. This time she would choose a partner in a serious, logical way, and would not be guided by her impulses. So she turned to treatment with Bach flower remedies for help, and started taking Chestnut Bud extract. Gradually she learned not to trust her impulses and intuition, as they always led her down the wrong path. She put her feelings and emotions to one side, and learned to rely more on her common sense and logic. She was finally able to see her recurring mistakes objectively and analyze the reasons for her previous failures. The intellectual gulf between her and her ex-husbands was now obvious to her. Things she had repressed began to surface, and she was able to review her life more sharply and clearly, from afar, as if she was looking at someone else's life.

Elizabeth decided to take a break from men and, for a while, she devoted her time to herself and her children. After a "cooling-off" period, during which she fully discovered the causes of her downfall - with the help of the Bach flower remedy - she began to date once more. She started a relationship with a man two years older then herself, a professional banker, who was the diametric opposite of her former brawny partners. He was tall and thin, a rational and reliable type with high moral standards. He was hardworking and ... square. But he had a sense of humor and loads of personal charm. She was in no hurry to get married this time, and finally "tied the knot" three years later. Her fifth marriage, which has lasted for eight years now, is her longest yet.

Extract 21

Mustard

Yellow

Aims to change: intense sorrow, melancholy, intermittent feelings of misery for no apparent reason, gloom that may be linked to certain hours or seasons.

Improves: long-term stability, sustained happiness, peace of mind which is not undermined by shocks.

A Complex Character

Guido was a regular sort of guy. Although he did not stand out at work, nor did he have any special talents, he was a good conversationalist and a dependable, well-liked friend. His wife of 10 years adored him, as did his two children. His life appeared to progress smoothly. However, every month, Guido was prone to unexplained and unjustified bad moods. They came on without warning, and he would withdraw into himself, shrouded in gloom, and become sulky and irascible, fly off the handle, and complain about anything and everything. He would become enraged and then immediately sink into despondency and cut himself off from his wife and children for a whole day. By now, his wife knew to wait for the storm to pass, and for Guido to become his old, lovable self again. His work colleagues were also familiar with these passing bad moods, but they accepted him as he was.

They invited all their relatives to celebrate the elder son's sixth birthday, and everyone arrived in high spirits. At the height of the festivities, Guido had one of his attacks of depression, and began acting obnoxiously. His wife asked him to go for a walk so as not to spoil the happy occasion, because she knew what was liable to happen when

Guido was in one of his moods. Guido refused. He had a temper tantrum and then became morose and withdrew into himself. He shut himself in his room and did not emerge until the party was over. His son was naturally distraught, as were the rest of the relatives, who had so much looked forward to the party. Instead of enjoying themselves, they spent much of their time taking turns going to Guido's room to try and coax him to come out.

The next day, when his black mood had lifted, Guido saw how his behavior had affected his son and resolved to put an end to his involuntary mood swings. He began taking Mustard extract, and every time he felt the "black cloud" approaching, he took the extract. Unprecedented tranquillity and peace of mind replaced his tantrums. He no longer plummeted into a state of depression or withdrew into himself for days at a time. His new-found well-being enhanced the quality of his own life and that of his family. The stability of his life was a novel experience for him, and he felt as if he were starting a new life.

Despondency
Martin was a closed, quiet, introvert type of man. He was not the kind of person who laughed out loud or displayed energetic behavior. As a child, his teachers and friends said that he had been born "sad." He was a serious character who went through life with a fixed expression of despondency. The corners of his mouth always pointed downward, like a sad clown. He was a diligent person, very thorough and "heavy." However, he was also creative and poetic, and liked to write poetry. From time to time, Martin experienced a feeling of heaviness, like a sort of depression, which would hit him right in the chest. He would become morose and lethargic for no apparent reason. He often wondered why he sank into bouts of sadness which were accompanied by gloom and heaviness. During these spells, he would find solace in writing poems. But sometimes his depression was so great that he could not see the point in carrying on living.

When he was 34, Martin realized he had to shake off the bad feelings and strange moods that beset him. He was convinced that they were the reason why he was still a bachelor. Who wanted a husband who was prone to such fits of depression? Eventually, he decided to take a Bach flower remedy, and started treatment with Mustard extract. Every time he felt a bad mood coming on, he would take the extract. The treatment helped him maintain an even keel over long periods of time, and he no longer sank into melancholy and deep depression. True, he wrote fewer poems than before, but he felt the improvement was worth the sacrifice.

Extract 23

Olive

Green

Aims to change: a sense of total exhaustion, lack of energy, the feeling that even the smallest of tasks is insurmountable.

Improves: renewal and growth, restoring energies, peace of mind, stability under pressure.

Return to Life

Edith suffered from severe migraines. They had started when she was 17 and increased in intensity, length and frequency as she grew older. Nothing helped - neither analgesic drugs nor various alternative relaxation methods like acupuncture, shiatsu, reflexology or exercise classes. Nothing reduced the intensity of the migraines.

Edith suffered terribly, and was completely incapable of functioning when she had a particularly bad migraine attack. She would stay in bed all day in total darkness, as any light made her condition worse. She would count the minutes and hours until her pain started to subside, leaving her feeling utterly exhausted, but at least free of pain.

Edith lived between attacks. During the interim periods, she lived in terror of the next migraine attack which would almost neutralize her and prevent her from living a normal life. So she was caught in a vicious circle: She was incapable of functioning when she was in the throes of a migraine attack, and was in the same state in between attacks, as the migraines left her exhausted and lethargic from the previous bout and pathologically fearful of the next.

She could see no way out of the vicious circle. She could not muster the strength to break out of it and try to realize her ambitions or objectives. She felt devoid of the essence of her strength. Even getting out of bed in the morning to face the new day sometimes seemed to her like an impossible task. Coping with everyday chores was beyond her, particularly if she felt an attack approaching. Edith's life was no life at all, and she knew she had to do something about it to improve her life between migraine attacks. She resolved to achieve a better quality of life, at least in the interim times. This would enable her to muster the strength to live a more or less normal life, and to reduce her fear of the next migraine attack.

Edith consulted with a Bach flower remedy practitioner and was treated with Olive. The initial feeling she had after beginning treatment was that, at long last, she was regaining her enthusiasm for little things that she had previously ignored. She felt that some of her previous vitality was returning to her, and that she was being recharged with new energies. For the first time in years, she felt happy. When she set herself a task, she now felt that she was capable of accomplishing it successfully. As time passed, the tasks became more difficult, and she accomplished them successfully too. Her basic self-confidence returned, and she felt able to rise to challenges and withstand pressures. She could function normally. She felt doubly strong: a physical strength she thought she would never have again, as well as an emotional strength.

Although her migraines did not disappear entirely, they occurred much less frequently and with less intensity. Edith felt that the improvement was a result of her sense of renewed strength and vitality, and she no longer feared the onset of another migraine. She began to come back to life.

War of Attrition

Sharon gave birth to her daughter when she was 24. Prior to the birth, she had been full of energy and very active. She had a full-time job with a firm of architects, and got home every day at five o'clock, at the same time as her husband. After a brief nap, they often went out to a movie, a cafe, a restaurant, or to visit friends. Her days were full and she enjoyed every minute. She liked her job and enjoyed the routine of her marriage.

After their daughter was born, Sharon's husband insisted that the baby needed the constant attention of her mother, and that no child-minder could provide her with maternal love and attention. Sharon disagreed with her husband, and wanted to return to work. She preferred to take a child-minder, if only for a few hours a day. It was important for her to dress up, get out of the house, and feel and look good. She wanted contact with people, and to combine motherhood with her personal desires. Sharon and her husband often quarreled about the matter until Sharon eventually succumbed, thinking that her husband may be right after all, and that she should devote all her time to her baby daughter - at least for the first part of the baby's life. She became concerned that if she went back to work she would be tortured by a guilty conscience, and that her heart (and her husband) would constantly remind her that she was not doing everything she could for her daughter. With some misgivings, Sharon decided to stay at home and look after the baby, at least for the first year.

As time went by, Sharon became increasingly frustrated with her new situation. Although she loved her daughter unconditionally, and gave her constant warmth and attention, she felt as if she were not doing anything for herself. She never even managed to read a book, and all her strength and time were devoted to looking after the baby. Sharon found that staying at home and taking care of the baby as well as doing the housework exhausted her physically. The absence of self-oriented activity and things she found satisfying drained her emotionally as well. She began to sleep a lot, and lost interest in things. She found it hard to do the housework, and she began to neglect it. She no longer bothered with her appearance, and shuffled around in her nightgown, unkempt and disheveled. She put on weight. Her life became a long, monotonous bore. Her daughter was her only source of happiness, the only ray of sunshine in her life. Besides that, Sharon was not interested in anything. She was always exhausted - almost to the point of the pathological - and nothing thrilled or excited her unless it was related to her daughter.

Sharon's husband watched his wife's condition deteriorate. He was caught on the horns of a dilemma. On the one hand, it was important for him that she continue looking after their daughter and not go out to work, but, in his heart of hearts, he knew that Sharon would be a changed person if she got out of the house occasionally. When the situation reached the stage that Sharon fell asleep regularly in front of the TV in the evening, the house was a shambles, piles of dirty laundry lay all over the place, and he could not remember the last time they had made love, Sharon's husband decided to encourage her to take herself in hand.

The couple had a frank discussion about things, and they decided that Sharon should go back to work. Now she had to look for a new job, as her previous one was no longer available. Sharon's condition was so bad now that she knew she had no chance of making a favorable impression on a prospective employer.

She consulted with a Bach flower remedy practitioner, and underwent treatment with Olive extract. Her zest for life began to return after a couple of weeks of treatment. Her tiredness, apathy and inability to cope with reality began to disappear. She was suffused with new energy, and felt that she was "coming back to life." Normal housework was no longer an impossible task for her, and she felt a sense of inner awakening. She felt that she could do whatever she wanted, and that nothing could stand in her way. The better she felt, the more she concentrated on her appearance. She bought herself new clothes, and when she felt ready to return to work, she was accepted for the first position she applied for. She was surprised and encouraged by this, and started working. Meanwhile, they found a devoted child-minder to look after the baby for a few hours a day. The extract enabled Sharon to take the first step toward physical and emotional recovery.

Extracts for the Treatment of Loneliness

Extract 14

Heather

Red

Aims to change: preoccupation with oneself, fear of being alone, inability to listen to others, garrulousness, tendency to bore others.

Improves: the ability to stop being selfish, willingness to help others, talking to the point rather than just rambling on.

Emotional Deficiency

Melanie's parents got divorced when she was nine years old. She stayed with her mother, who remarried and had two more children. From the day of the divorce, Melanie felt rejected, and later she felt that her mother clearly favored her two younger brothers from the second marriage, and that she did not pay Melanie any attention at all. Melanie never expressed her feelings to her mother, who was not an easy person, and was, in fact, a bit of a tyrant. She had a very clear perception of how things should be, and she demanded a lot from her daughter. Melanie lived in a constant rat-race of trying to prove herself and show her mother what she was worth, and how good her achievements were. But her mother took no notice of her endeavors and never told Melanie how much she appreciated her.

Melanie constantly felt the lack of emotional warmth. She felt neglected, and she perpetually searched for the warmth and love she missed so much. As she did not find them at home, she looked for them outside. As a little girl, she openly demanded her teachers' attention. Her classmates considered her the class pest. When she grew up, she looked for warmth in other ways. She would overstay her welcome at her girlfriends' houses, and had to be shown the door.

On her way home from school, she would talk to her friends about anything and everything just to prolong their time together and delay her arrival at home. When she reached adolescence, she started dating boys and slept with them without hesitation. All the local boys knew that Melanie was an "easy lay." She had a bad reputation. For her part, Melanie got from her casual relationships with boys what she lacked at home. The physical attentions of a boy were, for her, expressions of warmth and love - even if they only lasted a few minutes.

She would cling like a leech to anyone who paid her the slightest attention. As soon as someone started talking to her, she would not leave them alone for a minute, even after she had got the message that they were not interested in her. She chose to ignore this, and even insulting remarks did not deter her. She was the local pest, and the only ones who benefited from her behavior were the boys who had "a good time" with her, as they put it. They exploited the situation to the hilt. Melanie's conduct was the talk of all the mothers in the neighborhood. Eventually, the rumors reached Melanie's mother, too. She sat down with her daughter and they had a few serious talks about everything. Melanie's mother began to comprehend the enormity of the gap between the Melanie she thought she knew, and the young woman sitting opposite her. When Melanie's mother became aware of the lack of warmth and emotional support from which her daughter suffered, she was conscience-stricken, and immediately resolved to mend her ways, and to devote herself to getting Melanie back on track. To start with, she sent Melanie to a Bach flower remedy practitioner.

Melanie began to take Heather. Her physical dependency on others, and her obsessive need and desire to be loved and embraced began to decline. She did not pester people like before, and no longer forced herself on others who were not interested in her company. She began to take notice of the reactions of others around her, and took into consideration what they had to say to her. The feeling of loneliness subsided and, with it, the need to tell others everything she had on her mind, whether they were interested or not.

After a while, Melanie managed to spend more time on her own without becoming anxious about it. She discovered an interest in things she could do on her own. At the same time, she stopped sleeping around, and started to discern who was genuinely interested in her, and who was only interested in her because he knew she was "easy."

Her whole image changed and, although the process was long and tiring, others started getting to know a new Melanie, admiring her abilities and appreciating her as an independent, self-standing person.

From Punishment to Joy
Sam was 40 years old, unmarried, and lived with his mother, who was chronically ill and incapable of looking after herself. They lived off social security. The mother was house-bound in a third-floor apartment, and Sam took care of all her needs. He cleaned the house, did the shopping and took care of all the odd jobs and chores happily and with love. He was not the type of person who would neglect his mother. He was such a devoted son that he never went out to socialize with friends, and certainly did not go out with women. He had very little experience

with women, and the few times he tried his luck at dating ended so dismally for him that he gave up the idea entirely.

The thing he loved most was volunteering for the Civil Guard. This gave him the opportunity to spend long hours with other people, to go on long walks and to share his thoughts and problems with anyone who would listen during the patrols.

He could not stop talking about himself, his sick mother, his dreams and wishes, his narrow world, or his desire to get married. Occasionally, his partner would hint to Sam that he did not want to hear any more, but any attempt to divert the topic of conversation was to no avail. Sam just kept on talking about himself.

Anyone in the Civil Guard who had gone on patrol with Sam asked the patrol manager never to pair him with Sam again. Everyone knew that Sam was basically a good guy, and they all appreciated his volunteering spirit, but they tried to steer clear of him, as they found his company unbearable. The shift manager did not know what to do, or how to manage the awkward situation in which he found himself. When there was no alternative, it was agreed that the others would take it in turns to "suffer" Sam out on patrols.

One of the other volunteers, who liked Sam and wanted to help him, began to drop hints to him about changing his behavior and way of life, and getting out of the habit of talking about himself incessantly. He tried to make Sam aware of his problem. After the two had spent a number of shifts together, Sam started to get the message, and his partner referred him to a Bach flower remedy practitioner for treatment. He knew that even if it did not help, it could certainly do no harm.

Sam started taking Heather extract and, in time, began to notice his own garrulousness and his almost uncontrollable habit of talking about his problems to everyone. This awareness led him to start letting others also have their say and listening to them. He discovered he could learn from others, give advice, and have an interesting and, more importantly, two-sided conversation. The less he talked, the more he absorbed what others had to say. He became familiar with other people's problems, and saw that sometimes his own troubles paled into insignificance compared with those of his partners. His ability to listen and his release from his obsession to talk about his own troubles *ad nauseum* opened up a whole new world before him.

He began to be a pleasant companion, a conversation partner who was interested in hearing the other person's story rather than just spill his guts the whole time. He began to notice the difference in the way people related to him, and he felt good about it. His ability to communicate with others improved out of all recognition. He knew that his next objective was to find a woman to spend his life with. Now that his peers treated him so well, the task did not seem so daunting.

Extract 18*

Impatiens

Red

Aims to change: impatience, particularly with people with slow reactions, independent, quick to act, inability to wait, impulsive, reckless.

Improves: understanding and tolerance of oneself and others.

Making It to the Top

Arthur was the owner of a start-up hi-tech company. He was extremely ambitious, and devoted most of his time and physical and emotional resources to his work. During the week he had very little time for his wife and daughter. But even over the weekend, he spent hours on his cellular telephone and never missed a call that might be important for the future of his new company. He concentrated on work and not on his family over the weekend. He was immersed in activity and felt that matters were progressing as planned.

Arthur was not a pleasant person at work, and his employees did not always manage to keep up with the cut-throat pace Arthur had set. When that happened, Arthur did not conceal his dissatisfaction with them. As far as he was concerned, the rate of progress had to be maintained at all costs. It was not easy for the others. Arthur was practical, quick-thinking and analytical. Anyone who thought too slowly for his liking, or spent longer than Arthur considered necessary on a job, was summarily fired.

The rate of personnel turnover at the young company was very high, which did not contribute to its chances of success. The employees, who felt that Arthur was mistreating them, tried to talk to him about it, requesting that he slow the pace of work down a bit. They told him they could no longer keep up with his demands. But nothing helped. He was so determined to reach the top within the time-frame he had set, and was so enthusiastic about his goal, that he resolved that nothing would stand in his way, even if he had to fire employee after employee. The atmosphere at work became increasingly unhealthy. The employees who managed to stay the course felt burnt out and on the verge of collapse. After their attempts to talk to Arthur about it failed, they decided to talk to his wife. Maybe he would listen to her and change his attitude.

Arthur's wife, who had not been aware of the seriousness of the situation at work, and had only felt the deterioration at home, resolved to do something about it, come what may. She spoke to Arthur and explained to him in no uncertain terms that if he did not change his ways, both at home and at work, he would be on his own; she would leave him.

Arthur was stunned. He had not realized how far he had let things slide. He had no idea how much his behavior had affected his wife and daughter, and how much his impulsiveness had hurt his employees, who were obviously extremely devoted to him. He confessed that he was not too happy with his life - either on the professional or the domestic fronts.

He decided to take a break for a few days, at the end of which he opted for treatment with Bach flower remedies. He began taking Impatiens which, together with his wife's shock treatment, made him become more patient with people. More importantly, he gradually slowed the pace down. Eventually he felt he could take his time with others, and listen to them more patiently; even if they were not quite as quick-thinking as he was, it did not mean that their ideas were worth less than his.

He began to spend more time with his daughter without worrying about how he could be spending the time dealing with company issues. His ability to listen to others, and to have long talks with his wife, returned him to the world of "sanity." He rediscovered his ability to have fun, to enjoy a good movie or a vacation - things that had previously seemed to him "a waste of time." The atmosphere at work changed out of all recognition - proving that the man at the top determines the nature of the place. The quality of Arthur's life improved dramatically, as did the quality of his family's life and the creativity of his employees.

Part of the Family

Ian was director of one of the most important sections of the State Department. He was an outstanding personality - one who radiated authority and decisiveness. It seemed as if no one in the entire Department could match up to his cool-headedness. He gave an impression of supreme confidence; with him, things were in "good hands." However, he never delegated authority and only relied on himself. He was in charge, and every decision or request was referred to him. His subordinates never dared to contradict him, disagree with him or venture to make any comments about anything he said or did, even if they thought he was wrong.

Ian stayed at the office until late, and would joke that he was always the one who turned on the lights in the morning, and turned them off at night. His subordinates showed him a great deal of respect, but never attempted to get close to him, as they often did with each other. Ian had a sort of condescending attitude, an air of arrogance about him, which also deterred his subordinates from befriending him. For his part, Ian never became friendly with any of them; this never bothered him, and it never occurred to him to behave more warmly toward them - until his wife died.

During the period of mourning, all the employees in his section paid him condolence visits. For the first time, Ian realized that he had never had a regular chat about anything other than work with them before. In fact, he knew nothing about any of them other than the things he needed to know for work purposes. He was amazed to find that even after all the years they had worked together, he knew nothing of the personal lives of his subordinates, even the most senior among them - how many children they had or anything else.

There were some embarrassing moments and long silences when they visited him. Suddenly Ian was forced to make small talk with people with whom he had never talked about anything other than work. He did not know where or how to start. For their part, his subordinates did not dare to talk to him about trivial matters, and stuck to things relating to work.

For the first time, Ian realized that there was a great chasm between him and his subordinates, and that while they respected him, Ian felt that they did not really care about him or his predicament. No wonder, he thought; if I never showed any interest in them, why should they relate to me any differently?

This greatly bothered Ian, and he realized that he had been wrong to run the department like that all those years. He felt lonelier than he ever had in his life. His wife was no longer alive, and other than a couple of friends, he did not have anyone close to him - not even at work. It was all his own fault.

He decided to try a Bach flower remedy, and was treated with Impatiens extract and Water Violet extract. The treatment helped him put his resolution into practice - to listen more to his subordinates and to give them more leeway. He would listen to what they had to say, and would consider their opinions seriously, not just with a nod of the head as if he agreed with them, only to instruct them otherwise at a later stage. Gradually he began to open up to his subordinates and became understanding and patient with them. After they had visited him at his home during the mourning period, he permitted himself to inquire after their families, displaying an unprecedented interest.

At first, his subordinates did not know what to make of this new approach, and were rather suspicious. But, in time, the barriers between them came down, and relations between Ian and the others became warm and cordial. Not only were they happier than ever before to come to work in the morning, but the atmosphere in the office improved dramatically, and they felt that Ian really relied on them and, most importantly, listened to them. They responded in kind, and showered him with warmth and attention. Ian, who had lost his wife, gained a new, caring family.

Extract 34*

Water Violet

Purple/Reddish

Aims to change: leading a sheltered, distant life, haughtiness, superior attitude, excessively responsible and independent.

Improves: sensitivity, tranquillity, peace of mind, respect, nobility, sympathy, providing wise counsel.

Treating People with Respect

Brian was a brilliant man. He was very successful in the computer company for which he worked, and received a good salary. He liked working with computers, not only because of the technology, but because it meant he could sit in front of a computer screen all day without having to make small talk with anybody. He was close to being anti-social - except for his few close friends, whom he chose with care.

He was not talkative, responding laconically when he had to talk to anyone. Only when the subject was work-related did he speak enthusiastically and at length. It was only then that he felt he was not wasting his time. He thought most people were stupid. Watching TV was a complete waste of time as far as he was concerned, unless there was an important documentary or science or nature program on one of the cable channels. He always worked alone and never relied on anyone else. Not surprisingly, people thought of Brian as aloof, superior, arrogant, and a person who liked to keep to himself.

Brian's main problem lay in his relations with women. Whenever he finally managed to initiate a conversation with a woman and ask her out, he found it hard to maintain the "nice guy" act in order to charm her and keep the relationship going. He normally ended a relationship before it got off the ground, as he thought all the women he met were stupid.

Brian generally ate lunch in the company cafeteria, where he often saw a nice young woman to whom he was attracted. After making inquiries about her, Brian discovered she was a department manager in another division of the company on the floor above his. He tried to initiate a conversation with her, but failed. Every time he tried to get close to her, he felt that she was not in the least bit interested in him. His instinctive reaction was to withdraw into himself and to forget the whole thing. But this time, after he had finally met someone whom he really fancied, he decided not to give up so easily. He managed to sit at a table close to hers and to start a conversation with her. After a few days, she finally agreed to go out on a date with him.

It was the first time that Brian had felt true love. He was head over heels in love with this woman. He felt as if he was high, and could hardly believe it was happening to him. They had a good relationship, but Brian's arrogance and superior attitude bothered his girlfriend. She was incisive and immediately realized what sort of character he was. Although she loved him, she found it hard to ignore his condescending approach to others, sometimes to her friends, with whom he had become acquainted. It bothered her greatly, and she appealed to him to seek help.

Normally Brian would have ignored advice like that, but this time, he acted on it immediately. Brian had always been supremely confident about his own self-control and unerring ability to decide what was good for him and how things should be run. He had always made decisions independently. But now he knew that if this relationship was important to him, he must do everything to safeguard it. He surprised himself with his willingness to act upon his girlfriend's suggestion.

He started taking a Water Violet extract and, right from

the first week, he felt his attitude toward others changing. He started feeling respect for people whom he had previously dismissed as stupid, and discovered that their ideas were not so idiotic after all. He stopped belittling people and started to realize that he should respect others and accept them for what they were. He now became more pleasant, and was nicer to people, often even smiling at them - something he had never previously permitted himself to do. He even found himself initiating conversations with people about trivial matters that had been a total waste of time for him before. He began telling his girlfriend about things that had happened to him during the day at work - a real breakthrough.

Brian's partner felt the transformation and was amazed by the extent of the change in him and by his new-found openness. She was particularly delighted with the fact that Brian turned to her for help and support when he was faced with a difficult problem, whereas previously he had withdrawn into himself and agonized inside. He also began treating her friends with more respect. Now she knew she could accept him as a more complete person who related to his surroundings with awareness and consideration.

The Odd Bird

Erika is now 65 years old. She was the only daughter of Jewish political refugees who fled the persecution of the Nazi regime in Germany in the 1930s. They settled in Tel Aviv, which, although it was the most developed city in the country, was alien to Erika's mother, who could not get used to the life or the mentality there. She was unable to learn the language, or cope with the heat and humidity. Erika's mother mixed exclusively with other people from the same background, continued speaking German and dressing Erika, who was almost eight years old, in fancy European-style dresses. She sent Erika to a ballet school and piano lessons, as befitted people of culture. Erika was definitely looked upon as an odd bird. Although her father adapted to his new country, mostly due to the fact that he found work as a bookkeeper and came into contact with the locals on a daily basis, his family life had changed dramatically compared with the way they had lived in Germany.

After World War II, Erika's mother persuaded her husband to return to Germany. Erika was once again uprooted from her friends and went to live in Germany, where she grew up. However, she felt her parents had made a mistake, and was ashamed of what they had done. She was determined to return to Israel as soon as she was independent. When she graduated from high school, and felt mature enough to make her own decisions, she went back to Israel and settled on a kibbutz.

However, she was no longer the Erika of her childhood. Life suddenly seemed much more difficult than it had been. She was compelled to adapt to the less refined culture and to the rough-and-ready behavior of the native-born Israelis. She withdrew into herself, and became shy and guarded. She felt that she had come from a rich, abundant world, overflowing with culture. This caused her to relate to the Israeli "sabras" as less cultured than herself, and she adopted a superior attitude toward them. She found it hard to accept that they attributed little importance to the way they dressed or behaved, or the fact that opera, poetry and foreign literature had little significance for them. She thought they were shallow and superficial, and she found it hard to make friends on the kibbutz. For their part, the others around her sensed her condescending attitude; her tendency to keep to herself - also a form of aloofness - did not win her any friends either.

Erika had a hard time, and found it difficult to adapt, but she did not want to return to Germany. She resolved to stay the course and to try to become "one of the gang," and thought that if she could only rid herself of her natural tendency to look down on others, everything would turn out well.

A German friend with whom she corresponded advised

her to take a Bach flower remedy, and Erika began to take Water Violet extract, which helped her overcome her superiority complex. She began to open up to others around her and started getting closer to the native-born Israelis. She started to trust them and like them. The moment the barriers came down, she felt at home. There were many discussions between her and the others; they got to know her and found her interesting. Moreover, they were intrigued by the wealth of culture she possessed. After a while, she was appointed a member of the local culture committee, in this way successfully integrating into the social life of the kibbutz. She was grateful for the opportunity her new friends had given her, while they appreciated her talents and abilities.

Extracts for the Treatment of Hypersensitivity

Extract 1*

Agrimony

Yellow

Aims to change: emotional anguish hidden behind a cheerful exterior, concealing worries from others.

Improves: the ability to make light of anxieties, genuine optimism, a subtle sense of humor without hiding behind a facade.

The "Problem"

Alvin's eldest son was autistic. To begin with, he seemed to be the same as any other normal baby. It was only when he reached the age when babies normally start responding that his parents noticed there was something wrong with him. After various tests had ruled out the possibility of defects such as deafness, mental retardation and so on, the baby was diagnosed as autistic when he was a year old. He did not communicate with his surroundings, or respond to instructions or to people who spoke to him. He was locked in his own world. Sometimes he reacted strangely when he heard music he especially liked.

Alvin took his eldest child's autism very hard. He agonized inside, and this kept him awake for nights on end. He worried about what would happen to their son when he and his wife were no longer around to care for him. What did the future hold for him, and why did it have to happen to them? Day and night he was tormented by these questions. Despite his inner agony, outwardly he maintained a jocular disposition, sometimes even going over the top with his cheerful attitude. He was the center of attention at every party, and generally played the clown among his colleagues at work. He never let anyone penetrate his shell. Only his wife knew what lay behind his jolly, comical facade.

Others around him, who did not understand the extent of the tragedy, admired Alvin's optimism, and praised him for being strong enough to get on with life despite his problem at home. They could not imagine the mental anguish Alvin went through every day after he left work to go home in the evening to be with his wife and son.

By the time his son was five years old, Alvin's emotional state had greatly deteriorated. His son's condition had not improved. At social gatherings of parents of autistic children, he saw how much progress some of the children had made, while his son had not advanced at all, despite all their efforts and hard work. Alvin's wife saw his suffering and begged him to stop pretending that life was a breeze. She knew that if he stopped repressing his pain and revealed his true feelings, he would lighten his emotional burden. Alvin was willing to change his ways, but had no idea where to begin.

He consulted with a Bach flower remedy practitioner and starting taking Agrimony. As time passed, Alvin began to feel he could discard his permanent, happy-go-lucky clown mask, quit joking around and pretending, and act more naturally with his friends. When he felt depressed, they could clearly see it on his face; conversely, they also knew when he was truly happy. Initially, his friends were worried that something had happened to him, but they soon discovered that the opposite was true. They were finally privy to the "real Alvin," and he, for his part, began to share his troubles with those closest to him - something he had done only rarely beforehand. He discovered that his load was a lot lighter and that his stress level was lower when he revealed some of his pain, instead of pretending that "everything was OK" when it wasn't.

Those around him also learned to appreciate him and his sincerity more than ever before. Now that they had been allowed into his inner world, they felt they could help reduce his suffering by participating in it. It was easier to talk to him about what had previously and euphemistically been called "the problem." The quality of Alvin's life improved, even though he still found his son's condition difficult to accept. But his struggle, which once took place both at home and outside, was now much easier to bear.

Anything but Pity

While Malcolm was a member of a crack military unit, he was wounded in action. He did not remember much about the incident, just a blinding flash, machine-gun fire, and the screams of his wounded comrades-in-arms. He was just 19 years old when he suffered severe burns all over his body, and had his right hand amputated. Malcolm, who had been the local pin-up boy, was now a broken, disabled war veteran, with a scarred, monstrous-looking face and a prosthetic hand. He felt bitter towards the generals who gave the commands in a war that he could in no way justify to himself.

He had no idea how to cope with the new reality. When his friends came to see him in hospital, he did not know how to behave with them. The last thing he wanted from them was pity. He had always had a macabre sense of humor, and now he exploited it to the hilt. He often made jokes at his own expense and at that of his wounded comrades in the same hospital ward; nothing was sacred. He made quips about "lending a hand" by taking off his prosthetic hand and giving it to someone who needed help, or about a friend who had lost an eye who could "keep an eye" on something by taking out his false eye. He did all he could to amuse his visitors, just as long as they did not pity him. Although his black sense of humor may have helped Malcolm to relate to them, and to overcome his embarrassment and unease, it made the others very uncomfortable, and they did not know how to take it. It only made them feel even more sorry for him.

After a year of rehabilitation, Malcolm had to face real life and start coping with the everyday problems outside the hospital. He was afraid to relinquish his macabre sense of humor because he thought it would help him cope with the outside world. But he knew he had to come to terms with normal life, and that the sooner he did that, the better it would be for him. He felt trapped. On the one hand, he knew he would eventually have to take off the mask he had donned during his stay in the hospital, but on the other, he did not know how to cope without it.

Deep inside, Malcolm agonized. He felt that he was a victim of cruel fate, and he could not prevent himself from wondering why it had to happen to him. More than anything, he did not know whether he would ever find a girl who would love him, or if he would ever get married and have children. One thing he knew for certain: He would have to behave naturally and sincerely, and to drop the act of the funny, ironic guy who appeared to take everything lightly. He knew he would have to reveal his true self, otherwise he would not be able to go on.

When he consulted with a Bach flower remedy practitioner, he was treated with Agrimony. He began to open up - initially to those closest to him, in this case his parents, who spoke to him endlessly about his condition. His macabre sense of humor began to disappear, he dropped his cynical approach and his detachment, and started to share his feelings with others. Gradually, he began to reveal more and more of his tortured inner world, and to heed other people's advice - something he had refused to do before. He sometimes saw the sense in what they had to say to him, and he felt his emotional burden lightening. The more he shared his experiences, feelings and daily struggles , the more his life assumed a regular pattern, and he finally managed to adopt a more positive and good-humored attitude toward life without pretending.

Extract 15

Holly

White/Violet

Aims to change: the feeling of being unloved, jealousy, suspicion, hostility, vindictiveness, lack of affection for others.

Improves: generosity, love, tolerance, happiness unaffected by external conditions.

The Evildoer

Betty was personnel manager in a large government institution. She was responsible for entire divisions of staff and for the fate of hundreds of people. She decided who would work where, what their ranks would be, the criteria for their salaries, and even the floors on which various departmental offices would be located.

Betty had a finger in every pie in the institution. She knew what was going on, and she would summon staff members from different departments in order to hear the latest bits of juicy gossip and make sure she was "with it." She wanted to know who had fallen out with whom and why, and would even make mischief between the staff members by telling Person A trumped-up stories that Person B had supposedly told Betty about Person A. In this way, Person A would "spill the beans" and reveal all about Person B.

Betty was the terror of the ministry, and sometimes it seemed that she was less interested in the good of the employees than in the status and power inherent in her position. Staff members often left her office in tears, or conversely, with sparkling eyes, depending on Betty's mood of the moment. She would delay promotions, or promote certain employees out of turn - whatever she felt like doing. It is no wonder that she was not greatly loved by her colleagues at work, to say the least.

Her husband was quite the opposite of her. He was a solid, respectable public figure, but was known as a modest man who never sought the limelight. People could not understand what he saw in such a diabolical woman. Many people who suffered as a result of Betty's actions went to her husband to try to get him to do something about her. He was surprised every time he heard a new story about his wife's nefarious deeds at work. At home she was the perfect wife, a pleasant partner, and a wonderful mother to their three children. He loved her dearly and could not understand where the evil she displayed at work came from. All attempts he made to talk to her about it were to no avail. She refused to "talk shop" at home, and got annoyed every time her husband tried to bring up the subject.

Everything changed when their daughter turned 18 and it was decided she would work at the institution for a short while before starting college. They agreed they would not reveal that she was Betty's daughter so as not to get people's back up about her getting the position through her mother's influence, while many other youngsters seeking temporary jobs were turned down.

When she started work, Betty's daughter was stunned to hear the terrible things the staff members had to say about her mother. As they had no idea who she was, they spoke openly about the "bitchy personnel manager," sparing her no mercy. They even cursed Betty when her name came up in conversation. In addition to the gossip, Betty's daughter witnessed first-hand some of her mother's appalling conduct toward staff members whom she had befriended. She saw how her mother mistreated the workers, and was quite unable to reconcile the loving mother she knew at home with the tyrant she saw at work. She was horrified.

One day, she summoned up her courage to tell her

mother what the staff had to say about her, adding that she was not surprised that they talked about her like that, considering Betty's mistreatment of them. She told her mother she was actually abusing them. Betty lost complete control and slapped her daughter resoundingly across the face.

At that moment, she realized how she had been behaving and decided to seek help. She knew that one side of her personality, the side that came out at work, was full of hardness, jealousy, suspicion, lack of respect for others, and an inability to truly share in another person's joys if they were not a part of her family. She knew that this hostility and her inability to demonstrate kind-heartedness and affection toward others were likely to rebound on her much more severely with others than with her daughter. She decided to change her ways, take drastic measures, and adopt a positive approach toward others.

She started taking a Holly extract. Her behavior at work became less harsh, and she managed to control her vindictive feelings. Her impatience, intolerance and lack of respect for others were replaced by a sincere wish to share in their problems and troubles, to empathize with them, and to understand them. Suddenly, she felt a positive energy flowing between herself and the members of staff, and whenever she asked one of them to her office, the person would leave with a smile on his or her face. She was truly happy for them when things worked out for them. It did not take long for her to receive positive feedback. The members of staff could not understand what had caused her transformation, but they feared her less and less. Her image as an evildoer gradually receded, and they now saw her as a positive and humane person.

They never made the connection between the girl who had worked with them for a few months and the change that had come over Betty.

Unrelenting Vindictiveness

Dina had been married for thirteen years to the love of her life. She had fallen in love with him at first sight when they were still college students, and their love had blossomed. The couple married, had two children, and set themselves up financially. Their lives followed an orderly pattern. The children grew up and no longer required such close attention. Dina and her husband began to go out more to socialize and spend time in cafés. Sometimes they went out together, and sometimes separately with their own friends from work, or the health club, and so on. They seemed to lead good, full lives. But they never tried to break the routine which, although pleasant, was devoid of surprises or excitement.

Eventually they became weary of the routine. Dina's husband began an affair with a female colleague, and their relationship turned into a passionate expression of true love. One day, after Dina had become suspicious that something was going on behind her back, she surprised her husband and caught him red-handed in bed with his lover. She made some awful scenes, and her husband decided to leave her for his lover.

Dina was unable to accept the way things had worked out, and harbored strong feelings of vindictiveness, wild jealousy and hatred of which she never thought she was capable. She began to pester her ex-husband and his new wife by calling them on the phone and harassing them in any way possible, including making scenes in public, cursing them, and wishing them ill.

Dina found herself becoming obsessed with evil thoughts. She was possessed by bad feelings and a destructive inclination. She could not focus on anything else, and her quality of life deteriorated. Her children, of course, were the main victims. When she finally realized that she could not go on like this anymore, and that she had to snap out of it for the sake of the children, she decided to seek help in the form of Bach flower remedies.

She was treated with Holly extract and began to

rediscover her ability to show and feel love. Her negative feelings began to be replaced by positive emotions, and her hostility toward her former husband and his new wife decreased. She began to open up to the world around her and realize for the first time since she got married that there were a lot of nice, eligible men around whom she had previously not noticed because of her feelings of vindictiveness. Men started to seek her out, and her new-found positive attitude also reflected on her children, who were now much calmer and could resume their normal lives.

Extract 33

Walnut

Bright Red

Aims to change: the need for a defense mechanism against strong influences, particularly when a major life change occurs (middle age, moving into a new environment, etc.)

Improves: the ability to adapt to change, to stand up for one's beliefs, decisiveness and perseverance.

Drifter

Howard had grown up in a tight-knit religious community. As he matured, he moved away from his family's strong religious beliefs after deliberating long and hard about such basic issues as the essence of God and Godliness, the place of man in the universe, and so on. His break from religion was difficult and painful, but luckily for him, he found a foster family, far from his home town, that provided him with warmth and support as he completed the difficult transition. The secular world was a confusing place for Howard.

He did not know where to set his limits. This new world in which he found himself did not offer him the clear-cut boundaries with which he had grown up.

Here, he had to make his own rules. For three years, he went through life in a daze, not knowing where he belonged. He did not quite feel a part of his new environment, and was no longer a member of the community into which he had been born.

And so he drifted until he met a bunch of Hari Krishna devotees. Initially, he was attracted to them out of pure curiosity but, after a while, he joined them, and found himself once again enjoying the benefits of belonging to a cult. His world regained its clear-cut format where demarcation lines between good and bad, the important and the insignificant, were clearly mapped out for him. His role was clear, and he finally found himself in a framework with defined aims. The warmth he felt within the group offered him a refuge from the ephemeral life of the secular world. After spending a good few months with the cult, he decided that this way of life was not for him as it was too reminiscent of the religious community in which he had grown up. He left the group, but instead of his life taking a more stable path, he lost his way entirely and started flitting from one group of weirdos to another. He tried whatever he encountered: He was a member of an environmental group for a while, attended Rainbow meetings, and even joined an anarchist sect for a short time. Essentially, he was more confused than ever and had no idea which direction to take; he even considered returning to his home community. But he realized that if he wanted a fighting chance to achieve stability, he had to act quickly, before he was influenced by the next craze.

He turned to a Bach flower remedy practitioner for help, and was treated with Walnut extract and Scleranthus extract. Gradually he began to free himself of the need to identify with a clearly-defined belief and started to develop the ability to acclimatize himself to one environment for long periods of time without chopping and changing. He was now able to protect himself from influences that had previously swept him away, and he began to put down roots, to develop free thought and independence from those around him. The stronger he felt on the emotional level, the more he prospered financially and this, in turn, made it easier for him to stick to his guns. He no longer vacillated between changing, frivolous ideologies and ideas. His life's path was now clearer than ever, and he succeeded in forging his own way.

Little Things

Fern was a simple-minded woman. She was easily swayed and never held a clear-cut view of her own. She tended to nod in agreement with any opinion she heard if the person expressing the idea made a strong impression on her. She was capable of agreeing with the owner of the corner store, who complained about the rotten state of the economy, but she just as easily sided with her boss, who extolled the virtues of the current government's economic policies. She agreed with everybody.

Fern was also a devotee of TV commercials and the Shopping Channel. She drove her husband crazy by popping off to buy the latest washing powder or cleaning agent, by rushing off to some store that had just announced a sale, or by ordering a product advertised on the Shopping Channel, even if she had no use for it at all. She was obsessed with buying. Not only was their home packed with useless consumer items, but their bank overdraft had reached frightening proportions, and Fern's husband had no idea how they were going to cover their deficit.

Fern and her husband argued constantly and violently, and his pleas and threats were to no avail. Fern was caught up in an uncontrollable whirlwind of buying. Although she was aware of their growing overdraft, Fern was confident that her husband would sort it all out. What difference would it make if she bought just one more "little thing"? (They were always "little things.") When Fern's husband realized that neither gentle persuasion nor threats were having any effect on his wife's attitude, he decided she needed help to extricate herself and her family from the situation into which she had gotten them.

Fern went to a Bach flower remedy practitioner and was treated with Walnut extract. Her ability to control her actions gradually increased, she found it easier to resist the temptation to give in to every "bargain" advertised on TV; she became more discerning. She was able to look at herself from the outside, as if looking at someone else, and thereby learned where her weaknesses lay. As time went by, she gained more and more control over her immediate wishes and impulsive behavior, and learned to postpone gratification. She could now distinguish between her real needs and what was superfluous. At the same time, she began to stick to her own opinions and not follow others blindly. In the end, life at home returned to normal. Fern developed a stronger personality, and became more self-aware and - most importantly - responsible for her actions.

Extract 4*

Centaury

Red/Violet

Aims to change: weak will, tendency to denigrate oneself, inability to say "no," dependence, submissiveness, compliance with others in order to justify "doormat" behavior.

Improves: calm, insight, knowing when to assert oneself, maintaining limits of privacy.

No Longer a "Doormat"

Greg was obviously a genius. He was brilliant and had an IQ that qualified him for "Mensa." He was a very quiet man, shy, closed and taciturn, and had just a few close friends. After graduating from the faculty of computer sciences at college, he got a job with a large corporation.

At work, both his colleagues and his superiors were aware of his virtuosity and brilliance. Everyone knew that if they had a problem, Greg would sort it out. They often took advantage of his good nature, and he would stay at the office long hours in an attempt to solve other people's problems at the expense of his own work.

Greg was so retiring and modest that he never complained about his work conditions, his salary, or his status within the company. Anyone else with his abilities would have climbed the professional ladder to a higher rank and a much bigger salary. But because of his diffidence and his inability to initiate things and to stick to his guns, Greg was never appreciated as he should have been. Although everyone recognized his abilities, his willingness to help, and his agreeable nature, there were some who exploited him and even mistreated him. Because of his lack of drive and ambition, Greg remained a low-level employee; it suited his bosses to keep a man of his caliber on a relatively low salary. Others at his level would have demanded huge sums of money.

Greg's inability to stand up for himself, his shyness and his submissive nature eventually caused him to realize that he was being exploited. He felt badly done by and put upon, and this feeling increased in strength until he began to get angry with himself for not doing anything to improve his situation. But he was so used to his place of work that he never entertained any thoughts of quitting and looking around for another job. He knew that, with his bashfulness, he would find it hard to get used to another company with new colleagues and different work systems. He would probably have to start at a lower level with a new employer. He resolved to take himself in hand and to go for what he really deserved. He started taking a Bach remedy - Centaury extract - and his ability to try his luck and express his wishes improved out of all recognition. He began to stick up for himself and to overcome his innate shyness. He also saw that when he mustered the courage to say what was on his mind, even if he dreaded it at first, the others respected him more. This encouraged him to develop an independent mind and to set his own limits. During work hours, he refused to help others if it was not convenient. He learned to do something he had never done before: to say "no."

After a while, Greg felt confident enough to go to his superiors and to ask for a raise in salary and promotion, as he deserved. They agreed to all his requests, of course. Greg felt that he had finally attained an important and respectable position, and his entire philosophy of life altered. He knew he had removed the stumbling block which had been in his way all his life. Now there were more opportunities available to him. He felt that as soon as he changed the way he felt about himself, everyone else began treating him differently. Not only did he change inwardly - he changed outwardly too. The inner change was reflected in his outer bearing. His walk become more confident and his posture improved.

Not Just Donations

Beth was a shy and retiring person. She was so withdrawn that no one ever managed to break down the barriers to get close to her and make friends with her. She was a wonderful artist, and she communicated with the outside world through her paintings. Her works of art were beautiful, and she participated in exhibitions all over the country, sometimes even abroad. However, her breakthrough to public renown was not a result of her own efforts, but those of her only close friend, who had assumed the role of Beth's PR person. She recognized Beth's genius and considered any help she could give to publicize her work a sacred mission. If not for her friend, Beth would never have shown any of her paintings to a soul, let alone exhibited them abroad.

As interest in Beth's work grew, she began to receive more and more requests to exhibit her work locally and abroad, to appear on TV art programs, to attend cultural events, and to give interviews. She turned them all down outright. With her bashfulness, she could not contemplate facing the public, and certainly not through the media, which would have exposed her to thousands - if not hundreds of thousands - of people. Her friend's pleas were to no avail. She tried explaining to Beth that they were on the verge of an important breakthrough, and that the publicity that was being offered would bring her fame, not to mention fortune. Beth turned down opportunity after opportunity, not only to gain the worldwide recognition and fame commensurate with her talent, but also to become a wealthy woman thanks to her own efforts.

Eventually, Beth realized that she had to do something to change her attitude - but not under particularly pleasant circumstances. Her daughter contracted an incurable disease, and only a series of operations abroad could save her. That required a great deal of money.

She and her husband knew that they could only raise the necessary funds if they initiated a charity drive for their daughter. Beth's husband joined forces with her ever-loyal friend and implored her to do something to launch her career, so that she would be able to sell her paintings for prices that would enable them to finance her daughter's medical treatment without donations. Beth realized that the onus to make the next move was now on her, and that she could raise the funds if she agreed to appear in public and, consequently, to sell her paintings for substantial prices. She still received offers to appear at cultural events and to be interviewed, and she knew the time had come to take action.

She consulted with a Bach flower remedy practitioner and started taking Centaury extract. The shyness that had been the bane of her life began to yield to an ability to communicate with people and to be more outgoing than she had ever been. Her fear of exposure began to diminish, and she began to feel that she trusted herself and had something of importance to say.

Her objective helped her to overcome her natural instinct to withdraw into herself again. She began to venture out into the big wide world to present herself and display her talents. She knew that she was highly esteemed, and was gratified to see that she received positive feedback from the public. The interviews she gave to the media were very successful, and she began to smile, make jokes, and generally gain self-confidence. She became successful and famous, and was now a popular participant not only in TV art programs, but also in talk shows. Her paintings were now being sold for prices she had never even dreamed of.

Thanks to her exposure to the public and the extent of the sales of her paintings, Beth and her husband managed to send their daughter abroad for the operations, and saved her life. Although her daughter was slightly handicapped for the rest of her life, Beth had saved her life and created a successful career for herself in the process.

Extracts for Protection against Despair and Hopelessness

Extract 24

Pine

Brown

Aims to change: guilt feelings, a sense of worthlessness, a tendency to take the blame for other people's actions, self-reproach.

Improves: a balanced sense of responsibility, not dwelling on past mistakes.

Who's Guilty?

Celia was a single mother, bringing up her son on her own. She went through years of suffering and financial hardship. She kept two jobs going simultaneously to be able to pay the rent and provide her son with everything his friends enjoyed, like a computer and various extracurricular activities.

Celia did not live in the best part of town, but she constantly explained to her son the importance of getting a good education and ensuring a better future for himself than most of the children who lived in the neighborhood. She did her utmost to encourage him, helping him with his homework, buying him books and encyclopedias, and devoting most of her spare time to his welfare.

As her son grew up, Celia found it increasingly difficult to keep tabs on him, not only because of the long hours she worked, but also because he was an independent young man who did as he pleased. Celia's control over her son gradually decreased.

One day, out of the blue, Celia received a phone call from the police informing her that her son had been arrested on charges of using drugs, and that she was to go to the precinct immediately to post bail for him. Celia was stunned. Not only had she never imagined that her son might be involved with the type of youngsters who used drugs, but she had had no indication or hints of such behavior. She hoped it was a one-time mistake. After she released him from police custody, however, her son confessed that he had been using drugs for a long time and that he was an addict.

Celia was distraught and felt as if the world had collapsed around her. She went into a frenzy, tearing her clothes, pulling her hair and beating herself. She wept with such intensity that she eventually fainted. When she regained consciousness she was beside herself with grief and guilt feelings. The latter were unbearable; she considered herself alone culpable for her son's predicament - he had nothing to do with it. She, and no one else, was the cause of it. She thought about the way she had brought her son up, and blamed herself for not accepting a marriage proposal; the man could have been like a father to her son, then none of this would have happened. She thought that it might have been better had she not devoted so much time and effort to bettering their financial situation, and rather spent more time with her son. She felt she had not been sufficiently on the ball in recent years, and that she had allowed her son too much freedom.

Celia began to punish herself for what had happened. She stopped caring about her appearance, and no longer bought things for herself which she called "luxuries," such as food she liked. She stopped going out with her friends once a week. She agonized, and was consumed with guilt feelings. Celia's sisters watched her deteriorate daily, and began to be concerned. They had seen her invest so much in her son over the years, giving him so much more than she could afford; they knew that her son was much more to blame than she was for what had happened. He had been given so much and lacked for nothing; they had expected him to repay his mother in kind instead of letting her down so cruelly. Celia's sisters spoke frankly to her, in an attempt to convince her that she was not to blame, and that if anyone should feel guilty, it was her son. But nothing helped. Celia only agreed to one thing that they begged her to do: to undergo treatment with a Bach flower remedy. She started taking a Pine extract and began to pull herself together.

She started to see things more objectively and to understand that she was not the only guilty party. She asked herself searching questions about the past - whether she could possibly have done more - and was eventually forced to admit that she had done her best for her son, while he had not repaid her efforts in kind. She began to examine her situation from a different angle. It gradually dawned on her that she been playing the role of the martyr all these years by taking responsibility for other people's mistakes, and that this was the message she had relayed to her son. She began to regain her strength as the heavy burden of guilt started to lift. After a while, Celia began to feel that her life was more balanced, and that her strength was returning. She now had the tools to cope with reality and to help her son rehabilitate himself.

Another Angle

Sean was a senior officer in the tank division. Salt of the earth, he was a fighter, a serious man who always set an example for his men, adhering to the military heritage of his superiors and passing it on to his soldiers.

During a military exercise with live ammunition, two of his soldiers were wounded. Their injuries were serious enough for them not to be able to return to the tank division after their recovery. Although a tribunal of inquiry exonerated Sean of any direct responsibility for the incident, he shouldered the blame for what had happened, and his entire demeanor changed radically. He spoke little and began to mumble indistinctly to himself. His fellow officers knew what a responsible person he was and how much he took things to heart. They realized what a shock the incident had been for him. However, they were sure it was a temporary phase that would pass.

Sean could not get to sleep at night, and when he did finally fall asleep for a few precious hours, he would generally wake up with a start from relentless nightmares. He was certain that the accident could have been avoided had he deployed his forces differently.

His friends tried to convince him that he was not to blame, and that the force deployment had been a lot more complex than he thought. They tried telling him that the ones to blame were those found guilty in the hearing. But their words fell on deaf ears. Sean was convinced that, even if the tribunal had decided otherwise, he had not done his job properly, and he decided to quit the division - the worst punishment he could inflict on himself. His girlfriend, who saw him torment himself and knew how responsible a person he was, also knew that the army was his life. If he resigned, he would wither away before her very eyes.

She persuaded him to try a Bach remedy, and he promised he would not quit the division before completing the treatment. He started taking Pine extract and, before long, he began to see things in their correct proportion. He now started to analyze the military exercise from a different angle. Suddenly he became aware of things he had not noticed before, things that had not occurred to him. He realized that by taking too much responsibility on himself, including responsibility that belonged to others, he was jeopardizing himself. He could now see that he was not the only one to blame, and began to examine the picture from an objective rather than a subjective point of view. He discovered he had been wrong to assume all the responsibility, thus letting other people off the hook. Some of the responsibility should go to them, and he should not shoulder all the blame. Once he had become aware of all this, his whole outlook changed, and he realized there was no reason for him to leave the division - much to the relief of his girlfriend and his comrades-in-arms.

Extract 29

Star of Bethlehem

White

Aims to change: fear of bad tidings, deep distress, physical and emotional trauma.
Improves: purity of body, mind and thought by freeing oneself from tension and trauma.

Getting Over Shock

Ron lost his leg in a serious road accident. It happened just before the completion of his tour of duty in an elite combat unit. He had hitched a ride with a young woman, who tried to overtake a truck and had collided head-on with a car coming in the opposite direction. She had been killed on the spot, while Ron suffered superficial damage all over his body. He also lost a leg.

He had been certain that if anything bad were to happen to him, it would be in battle. He could not believe that he had been injured in a road accident just before finishing his military service, that he had lost a leg and that his life had changed forever. He was in total shock and could not take it all in. He kept asking himself: "Why me?" and "Why did it have to happen just a few weeks before the end of my military service?" He was not interested in anything else, and was incapable of understanding the implications of his injury. He lay in his hospital bed, staring into thin air and mumbling unintelligibly to himself. He slept a lot. He seemed to be in a different world and, at times, did not exactly know where he was or what had happened to him.

Ron's mother began treating him with Star of Bethlehem extract in order to help him snap out of his initial shock. She mixed the drops into his morning tea, and Ron's recovery began from the very first day. The effect was almost immediate. Ron began to become his old self again, and to speak coherently. He began to comprehend what had happened to him and what the future held in store for him. The extract helped to stave off serious depression and feelings of self-pity. He was able to view his situation clearly and in a balanced manner, and to assess the difficulties with which he would have to contend. He attained a state of emotional balance much more rapidly than the doctors had imagined, and the path to rehabilitation was much easier than expected. In comparison with other amputees, Ron learned to use the prosthesis very quickly, and started walking on two legs. He started to function normally again, and his emotional scars were minimal. He resumed his regular life and left the trauma and stress behind him.

The End of the World

Heidi was 29 years old and about to get married. Most of her girlfriends were already married, and she had started to worry that she would be left on the shelf. So, when she finally met the love of her life, she was the happiest person in the world.

Her husband-to-be was an adventurous type. He enjoyed dangerous sports, going on jeep treks, and engaging in rappelling, free-fall parachuting, and anything that smacked of danger.

Two weeks before the wedding, Heidi's fiancé went abroad with two friends to go rafting on a major river in Africa. He never returned from that adventure. The boat he and his friends were in was swept away by a roaring current and overturned. Heidi's fiance's head hit a rock, and he was killed instantly.

Heidi received the terrible news at home, when her fiance's mother phoned her. Everything went blurred and then black, and Heidi fainted. When she regained consciousness, she could not shake off the feeling of failure; she felt that her world had collapsed around her, and that she had nothing left to live for. Her trauma and shock were extreme, and for a while, she could not function properly.

In an effort to resume her normal life, Heidi began to take a Star of Bethlehem extract and gradually began to recover. Although the Bach remedy was no comfort, she no longer plunged to the depths of grief and despair she had previously reached, and she was ultimately able to view things clearly, and not see everything with such finality.

After a long period of rehabilitation, Heidi managed to get back to a more or less normal routine. She continued with the treatment, as she had not yet gotten over another trauma: Two years after the accident, she was still afraid to answer the phone because she was terrified of receiving more bad news. In fact, she hated the instrument. She only used it if she had something really important to say.

Heidi continued taking Star of Bethlehem extract for a long time until the trauma began to diminish. She only stopped taking it when she felt she had reached a state of equilibrium and was strong enough to manage without it.

Extract 30

Sweet Chestnut

Green

Aims to change: a feeling of reaching the end of one's tether (although not to the point of feeling suicidal), the inability to see the light at the end of the tunnel.

Improves: the belief that unbearable suffering is a vital experience and that suffering brings strength.

The Affair

Sandy was 45 when her world came to an end. She was happily married to a successful businessman who was a partner in a large company. They had four children and were very wealthy. They indulged in luxuries that other families could only dream of: living in a huge mansion in an up-market area, going abroad several times a year to exclusive resorts around the world, and dining at the best restaurants. Money was never a problem for them. One day it all came to an end when detectives knocked on Sandy's door and arrested her husband on charges of large-scale embezzlement.

Sandy's life was in turmoil. Her husband spent a long time in prison awaiting the court ruling, and he was eventually sentenced to thirteen years' imprisonment. Not only had her husband been taken from her and her children, she now had to run the family affairs single-handed and cope with the reactions of the members of her social circle. The articles in the papers and the great publicity they generated caused Sandy and her children a great deal of painful embarrassment. People would point to them in the street and the children were taunted in school. There were incidents of actual abuse.

Sandy not only suffered her own torment, but she also experienced her children's anguish and humiliation as if they were directed at her personally. The suffering was intolerable, and Sandy had no idea where she would find the strength to carry on. The only thing she kept repeating to herself was that collective memory was short and that, after a while, everything would die down and people would lose interest. But, despite this idea, which helped preserve her sanity, the experience she was going through was almost unbearable. Her brothers and sisters-in-law stood by her, encouraging her and the children constantly. This played an important part in keeping Sandy going, but she felt she was close to a nervous breakdown.

There were days that she would spend long hours in bed staring into space, or sleeping for hours as an escape from reality. The most difficult part for her was watching her children suffer, and trying to encourage them when she herself felt that she had come to the end of her tether. She also felt a tremendous amount of rage toward her husband. Not only had he betrayed his colleagues at work, but also - and especially - his family. She thought that if he had considered them, he would not have acted in the way he did. But it was too late to turn the clock back. Sandy knew she still had to contend with her husband. All this left her feeling emotionally drained; her reserves of strength were dwindling, and she had nothing to lean on.

Realizing the severity of her situation, she decided to consult with a Bach flower remedy practitioner. She began taking Sweet Chestnut, and the extract helped her realize that her situation was temporary. She found the strength to carry on. Her point of view changed, and she adopted an optimistic approach. She began to concentrate on what she had left - namely, her children, and her supportive extended family - rather than on what she had lost. She started relating to her predicament as a positive, character-forming experience. She knew that if she was patient and gave herself time, she would get over this crisis and would be better able to handle crises in the future. She knew she would go through a difficult period, but the extract enabled her to carry on the struggle, find new reserves of strength for it, and adopt a more optimistic approach.

A Dutch Tourist

Danny grew up in a village in a Mediterranean country. After graduating from college, he decided to try his luck in the city in which had studied. However, things did not go too well for him there, so he decided to return to his village. A few months later, he met a Dutch tourist, and it was love at first sight. They got married soon afterward and settled into the routine of a happy marriage. Danny worked on a farm, and his wife found a job in an office in a nearby town. Two years later, they had a baby girl, and Danny was besotted with his gorgeous little daughter. He showed her off whenever he could, and spent every spare moment with her. He built her special games and toys out of wood.

However, Danny's wife began to find village life dull and boring. She had come from a city in Holland and began to miss the excitement and hustle and bustle of an urban environment, as well as her parents and other relatives. Danny watched as his wife lost her zest for life. They discussed the problem repeatedly, in a genuine attempt to find a solution such as moving to a big city, but in time Danny's wife began to express her wish to return to Holland openly and forcefully. Danny knew he could never leave the village or live in a country with a different mentality and a language he could not speak. And he was loath to uproot his daughter from her familiar surroundings and take her away from her grandparents. Their discussions turned into ugly arguments, and usually ended with one of them storming out of the house and slamming the door behind them.

One day, Danny returned home to find the house empty. His wife had left him a note saying that she had taken their daughter back to Holland with her. Looking around, he saw that the clothes closets were empty, and all the toys were gone. Danny was stunned and felt as if he were on the point of passing out. He collapsed on the bed in disbelief. How could his wife do such a thing to him? More than that, he was angry with himself at not having noticed that his wife was preparing to leave. The thought of his little daughter and the desire to hold her in his arms were excruciatingly painful. He felt as if he was having a total breakdown - physical and emotional.

He felt helpless and devoid of strength, as if all his blood had been drained from him. He did not know where he would find the strength to cope with the situation. He had formulated a plan and deep down knew what he had to do now, but he could not muster the strength to implement it.

He did not leave the house for three straight days. He was in total shock and traumatized by his wife's departure. His entire world had collapsed around him. Even in his worst nightmares, he had never imagined his wife leaving him in such a way. He loved her and their daughter madly.

Various scenarios crossed his mind, confusing him completely. Perhaps his wife had fallen in love with someone else, and had been having an affair behind his back, and that was why she had left the country. Something might have happened to the little girl; or his wife may not allow him to see his daughter anymore. The longer he thought about the whole thing, the more desolate his world became. He wallowed in misery and became weaker and weaker. Even his breathing became labored.

After three days of isolation, he began to pull himself together, and resolved to muster the strength to carry on. He knew that the situation could be solved and that he had to do anything he could so that at least he could see his daughter again. But he did not know where he would get the strength to carry on. He decided to consult with a Bach flower remedy practitioner, and was treated with Sweet Chestnut. The extract enabled him to find the strength to carry on and leave the trauma of the past behind him. He was now able to recover from the initial shock and to collect his thoughts in a clear and orderly way, so as to cope with the situation. Danny overcame his feelings of failure, as well as his emotional exhaustion and weakness. He now felt able to act logically and to implement his plans, rather than rely solely on instinct. With his renewed strength, Danny was confident he would be able to win his wife and daughter back.

Extract 38

Willow

Light Green

Aims to change: harboring resentment, bitterness, a feeling of being badly done by, and feeling miserable.
Improves: greater optimism, less bitterness.

Bitterness

Irene immigrated to the United States from Russia with her parents when she was 11 years old. She adapted to life in her new country quickly and made many friends, although she never quite managed to rid herself of her foreign accent, even after many years in the U.S. Her parents, on the other hand, found the transition very difficult, although they eventually settled into new jobs and even found a circle of Russian emigrés with whom they socialized and spoke Russian. Irene was a devoted and obedient daughter, the kind of child any couple would have wished for. As the first member of the family to learn English, she helped her parents to adapt to their new country, read important documents to them during their initial period in the U.S., and explained the various procedures they had to undergo. They could never have managed without her. Irene's parents were very proud of her, and they never stopped singing her praises to all and sundry.

When Irene was 16, she fell in love with a neighborhood boy who was a few years older than she. He was of Sicilian origin, olive-skinned and wiry. He only had a high-school diploma, but he sold computer printers and made a good living. Irene's parents did not like the idea of their daughter dating a "dark-skinned man," and they begged her to leave him. When that failed, they made her life a misery by means of family sanctions, punishments, and so on. They made it clear to her that she was letting them down, and that they expected better of her. They hoped that she would fall in love with someone who was at least well educated, and, better still, an ex-Russian like themselves. But nothing helped. Irene married her boyfriend as soon as she turned 18. Her family ostracized her and severed all ties with her. Soon after she got married, Irene became pregnant and gave birth to a boy. The couple ran the successful business together, and loved each other very much. Irene's family did not renew contact with her; they never met their grandchildren.

After ten happy years of marriage, and the birth of two more children, Irene's husband died of cancer. Only three months elapsed between the diagnosis and his death, but they were the three hardest and most painful three months of Irene's life. She was left a widow, with three children and no support from her family. She was alone in the world.

When Irene's parents heard about her tragedy, they went to visit their daughter and renewed the relationship. In her sorrow, and in the absence of any other consolation in the world, Irene forgave her parents for all the years during which they had ostracized her. Irene's parents got to know their grandchildren and, as far as they were concerned, the family was reunited. But, despite having forgiven her parents for their behavior toward her, Irene was unable to conceal her bitterness and the deep-seated grudge that she bore. Over the years she had harbored feelings of rage, resentment and bitterness toward her parents. She could not just let bygones be bygones. She had always been the devoted model daughter who had cared about her parents and helped them as much as she could, and had been treated disgracefully by them.

She became a hard, bitter woman. She complained about everything, and nothing satisfied her. Everyone suffered - her parents and, in particular, her children. She behaved as if the whole world was against her, as if she had been used or cheated. She wanted revenge, but she did not know exactly against whom. She was so immersed in her own private suffering that she entirely neglected her duties as a mother. She never took her children on excursions, or did anything to give them a better life. She just fulfilled the most basic maternal obligations.

The children suffered greatly from all this. Not only had they lost their father, they now felt they were losing their mother as well. In the absence of a proper domestic framework, the children went wild. Their behavior changed drastically, both socially and at school. After their academic performance deteriorated significantly, the school principal asked Irene to come see her and the social worker. Irene suddenly realized that she had to do something about the situation, and change her attitude.

In addition to the plan of action that Irene formulated together with the social worker and school principal, she decided to undergo treatment with a Bach flower remedy. She started taking Willow extract, and the effect was almost immediate. Irene became less pessimistic, and started looking at the world more positively. She stopped griping and complaining the whole time. She became more involved in the children's lives, asked how their day at school had gone, and what homework they had, and they gradually allowed her into their personal lives and shared their thoughts and problems with her.

Irene's feeling of chronic bitterness gave way to a *joie de vivre* that she had not felt since before her husband's illness. She and her children began to function as a family again and their lives returned to normal. The children's schoolwork improved immediately, and the positive feedback Irene received convinced her that she was succeeding in living an emotionally healthy life. She felt she had finally effected a reconciliation with her parents, and she resumed a full and peaceful life. For her, resentment and anger were now a thing of the past.

"Sourpuss"

Cassandra never had a good word for her friends, her work colleagues or the members of her family. She hardly ever said "thank you," and never praised anyone for their achievements. She was always complaining and moaning, and had plenty of gripes against everyone around. That was why she had an office on her own at work. Everyone complained about her to the boss, saying she was impossible to get on with. They even nicknamed her "Sourpuss" because she was such a bitter and dissatisfied person.

She was in her fifties, an "old maid." Her mother died when she was 42 and, until then, she had lived with her in a small apartment. Her father had died when she was a small child, and she felt that, as an only child, she could not leave her mother on her own so that she could go out and lead her own life. She felt an enormous sense of obligation toward her mother, and lived in its shadow until her mother died of old age.

Cassandra felt that she had missed the boat. Deep inside, she knew that she would never get married. She was heartbroken about it, and it made her very hard and bitter. Her colleagues at work knew of her predicament, and whenever there was an incident at work involving Cassandra, the others would say: "Mind you, it's no surprise, considering the life she's had." One day, Cassandra was walking along the corridor at work when she heard two women discussing an incident in which she had been involved earlier in the day. The two ended their chat with the regular closing remark: "Mind you, it's no surprise, considering the life she's had..."

The sentence echoed in her head incessantly and relentlessly for several days. She heard it before she went to sleep at night, in the morning when she awoke, and at work. The words were a kind of mirror for her, which allowed her to view herself objectively for the first time. Suddenly, she realized that she was truly unbearable.

Her strong desire to change led her to consult with a

Bach flower remedy practitioner. She was given Willow extract and began to feel an improvement right from the first weeks. She realized that she had been behaving like a "chronic moaner" who always had something to complain about. Nothing was good enough for her. She began to view life from a different perspective. She began to understand that only if she took the initiative and effected a change in her life, was there a chance that she could change. She started looking at life more optimistically, and began to rediscover her zest for life. She began to pamper herself and allow herself a few luxuries that she had never had before. She saw that there were pleasures in the world that could make life easier, and change one's perspective.

Cassandra began to smile at people, and say a good word from time to time - things she had never done before. As a result, the others began to relate to her differently, more positively. The process of change was gradual, but ultimately Cassandra was a changed woman. People saw her in a different light, and she was capable of giving of herself. Her life was no longer so terrible; she discovered that it also held some pleasant surprises, and that if one smiles, one receives a smile in return.

Extract 22

Oak

Green

Aims to change: normally strong but lacking the courage to fight sickness or combat distress.

Improves: courage, the ability to fight without losing hope, stability.

Unbreakable

Victor was a strong man. He was tall and well-built, and had the muscular shape of a bodybuilder. He attributed great importance to his masculine look, and he worked out mercilessly in the gym to maintain his trim figure. He ran for miles, always testing his endurance level and his physical abilities.

Psychologically, he was also a fighter. He never gave up easily and stuck to his views and principles. It was very hard - sometimes impossible - to sway him or to persuade him to see a different point of view or change his line of action. He was so stiff-necked, decisive and inflexible that sometimes his stubbornness appeared pathetic. He was the classic macho type, and enjoyed huge success with the opposite sex.

He went out a lot and dated a great many women. They were easy prey for him; his alluring looks and blatant masculinity made women fall into his arms. For his part, he made the most of his looks and changed his women on an almost daily basis. He was an amazing performer in bed, and made every woman he dated feel that she was the only woman in his life.

His carefree bachelor days lasted a long time, but ended abruptly when he began to feel something was wrong when he urinated. Every time he went to the bathroom, he felt discomfort when he urinated. After two weeks, he noticed a discharge from his penis. Victor's imagination ran amok, and he thought of all the worst-case scenarios, from some strange and awful venereal disease to cancer. He consulted with a doctor immediately and was diagnosed as having gonorrhea, a common sexually transmitted disease - especially among males. He was immediately treated with antibiotics and injections.

Victor was shocked that he had contracted a sexual disease. He went through a period of crisis, a sort of psychological breaking-point. He, the great macho, had never imagined that something like this could happen to him. More than anything else, he felt extremely embarrassed that it had. He could not convince himself that, after so many sexual encounters without contraceptives, it was only to be expected. He thanked God repeatedly that he had not contracted AIDS, and consoled himself with the thought that his disease was curable. Above all, more than the feeling of embarrassment and unpleasantness, he was sorry he had been careless and had not taken protective measures. On the one hand he felt that he had been let off lightly, but he could not shake off the thought: "Why me?"

Victor knew that not only did he have to change the pattern of his sexual activities and be more careful, he also had to alter his psychological make-up and approach radically. He realized that it was his own conduct that had led to the psychological state in which he found himself after discovering that he had contracted a sexual disease.

He decided to consult with a Bach flower remedy practitioner and was treated with Oak extract. The treatment enabled him to delve more deeply into his own personality, and he felt he could be more lenient and flexible with himself occasionally, less rigid and stubborn. It was no longer so important for him to maintain the image of a strong "invincible" character, and he started showing uncharacteristic affection for other people. He learned to be less decisive and to listen to other people's opinions; he even succeeded in adopting different ideas and examining options that had not appealed to him previously. Life was now easier for him, and he saw that the world did not come to an end if he admitted he was wrong. Ultimately, Victor was easier on himself and on other people, and the tough image he had previously nurtured gradually mellowed.

The Shock of Her Life

Jenny was a senior manager in a large conglomerate. She had reached her position as a result of hard work and assertiveness. She would put people in their place and never let anyone pull the wool over her eyes. She had gained a reputation as a tough, strict yet very efficient manager. She abhorred working with people whom she thought did not pull their weight, and she fired employees frequently. The staff members who survived in her department were efficient, quick-witted and very well organized.

Jenny's charismatic personality affected everyone in the department. They did everything to please her, and to squeeze a compliment or a good word out of her. If a member of staff received a pat on the back from Jenny, he or she would be elated. It meant that they were doing a very good job. But because of her high standards of efficiency and perfection, Jenny often treated her workers with contempt or irritation, even if she did not always mean to do so. She often gave that impression unintentionally. She would let loose on a staff member for no apparent reason, or make peculiar demands, and then explode if things were not done to her liking.

One day, one of Jenny's most diligent staff members went to Jenny's office to report that she had completed a long-term project she had been working on. She was one of Jenny's best and most highly esteemed employees in the department. She waited patiently and silently in Jenny's office while Jenny spoke at length with a customer on the phone. No sooner had Jenny put the phone down than she began to shout at the hapless employee with unrestrained rage for no reason at all. The shocked woman had no idea what she had done wrong, and why she deserved this stream of invective. She left Jenny's office stunned and confused.

The other members of staff who had witnessed the scene decided that this time Jenny had gone too far. They resolved to go talk to her, and held a lengthy discussion with her during which they made it clear that they were not willing to tolerate such behavior any longer, and that she sometimes forgot that they were merely human beings. They informed her that they had several courses of action at their disposal, and that the union was on their side.

This time, it was Jenny who got the shock of her life. She returned home shaken by the talk with the union representatives. She knew she sometimes acted out of line and went a bit overboard, but had no idea of the extent of the effect she was having on the staff members. She resolved to change her ways, and went to a Bach flower practitioner for treatment.

She was treated with Oak extract and began to be act in a more restrained manner. Her reactions were less aggressive. The change came easily to her. She managed to slow down her intensive pace at work, as it did not get her farther, but just shortened the process a bit. She began to demonstrate more respect for her workers, and became more pleasant, tolerant and patient. Even her facial expressions became softer, and she no longer felt that she was "Superwoman" in the office. She began to realize that she would never have got to where she was without the help and support of her colleagues in the department. She started to express this newfound appreciation to her staff, and the whole atmosphere at work changed. The employees now worked with joy and love, and were treated with affection, understanding, and - most importantly - respect by Jenny.

Extract 10

Crab Apple

White

Aims to change: a feeling of being physically and mentally impure, the inability to connect up with one's destiny, with oneself or with others.

Improves: broader horizons, openness, pure self-satisfaction, cleanliness and purification.

The "Defect"

Lily had long light brown hair with a long fringe which covered her forehead. She never tied her hair back in a ponytail, or put it up with pretty barrettes, which would expose her face and neck. The reason was simple: Lily was ashamed of her ears. She was convinced she had been born with "elephant ears," and always made sure they were covered. She would comb her long hair forward to cover the "defect" of which she was so ashamed.

Lily's mother and two sisters could not understand what she was on about. They did not think her ears were exceptionally large or protruding. While they were not very small, she certainly had nothing to be ashamed of. When Lily was in her teens, they let her be, thinking that this craziness would pass. But it did not, and no amount of persuasion and coaxing by the members of the family, including her father, helped.

She was determined to undergo plastic surgery in order to solve the problem once and for all. Her family was very surprised when she revealed her plan. They knew Lily suffered from the self-image she had developed, but they had no idea that it bothered her to that extent. They considered the idea of plastic surgery ludicrous. Her mother strongly objected, as she saw no justification for it. However, when she saw how determined her daughter was to have the operation, she persuaded her to consult with a Bach flower remedy practitioner first.

Lily was treated with Crab Apple extract, and she began to view herself and her surroundings differently. She began to feel less exceptional, and attached less importance to how others saw her. Her "defect" began to recede. The moment she no longer cared what others thought of her, she thought she was more beautiful than ever before. She began to perceive herself differently, and gradually began to tie her hair back, initially with barrettes and bands, and eventually in a French braid. She received compliments from her family and friends on her new look, and they asked her where she had been hiding all these years, and why she had never shown her beautiful face all this time. Lily was totally taken aback with the intensity of the response, and she was flattered. Her self-confidence increased and she would spend a long time looking at herself and admiring herself in the mirror - something she had never done before because of her "ugly ears." Her view of the world changed completely and she never mentioned plastic surgery again.

Coming Clean

Bob had been a drug addict for many years. He had tried unsuccessfully to kick the habit on his own many times, and eventually ended up at a drug rehabilitation facility that combined treatment with agricultural work. The facility was located in a beautiful area and, in the fresh country air far from the dust of the city and the drug dealers, Bob was rehabilitated. It was a long and torturous process, and Bob went through a lot of pain and crises, both physical and emotional. After he had been clean of drugs for a year, he left the farm with a view to resuming normal life.

He left the city in which he had lived previously and moved to a town in the north of the country where he found a job at a boarding school as a youth leader for disadvantaged youngsters. He liked his work and made new friends among the other youth leaders. None of his colleagues had ever used drugs, and most came from a very different background than his.

Although he got on with everyone, he felt there was something rotten inside him, and that he could poison everything and everyone around him. He never managed to shake off the image of the guy he had been for so many years - the former drug addict with a tainted personality who did not take care of himself and who would do anything to get hold of his next fix. His former image haunted him and he knew that that guy, the drug addict, was stalking him everywhere. He knew he had to be on his guard day and night, and that the battle against slipping back into his former habit began afresh with every new day. Although he was living in a different environment now, he knew how easy it would be regress into his old ways. First and foremost, the thing that bothered him was the feeling that he was like a blight wherever he went. Even if people did not relate to him like that, or were unaware of his past, he felt as if he were the carrier of a disease. Although he thought that time would help, and that the feeling would disappear, he was still afraid of what might happen if he slipped up.

One of the instructors at the rehabilitation facility who kept in touch with Bob told him about Bach flower remedies, and recommended that he try them. Bob began treatment with Crab Apple extract, and gradually, during the first few weeks of treatment, started to feel as if he were being cleansed of those bad thoughts. The sense of being impure and of carrying something unclean inside him began to fade. He felt as if he were actually being reborn. He gradually severed his last ties with the past and began to build his new world with a feeling of cleanliness and purity. The remedy freed him of the bonds he had thought inseverable. He was now able to expand his horizons, undertake new things, and undergo new, undreamed-of experiences. He now enjoyed experiences like taking walks in the country, bathing in springs and horse-riding, in a way he never imagined possible. Now that he was emotionally free of his traumatic past, he could enjoy the pleasures of the new world which had opened up before him.

Extract 19

Larch

Dark Red

Aims to change: sense of insecurity, anticipation of failure and fear of success, not trying to succeed, lack of belief in abilities, inferiority complex.

Improves: willingness to try, faith in one's abilities, great perseverance, steadfastness.

As Good as the Next Guy

Penny grew up in a small, underpriviliged southern town. Born to a family of immigrants, she was a gifted child, bordering on genius. When she reached high-school age, she was sent to a special boarding-school for gifted children on the East Coast. There were quite a few other children from disadvantaged neighborhoods, who had been sent to the school in the hopes of "making something of them."

Penny was a dominant figure in her class, which consisted of both boarders and students from the nearby town. She was very bright, and enjoyed success both at her studies and socially. As the student population was integrated, she did not feel discriminated against and had no sense of inferiority whatsoever. After graduating from high school, Penny applied to several Ivy League schools and, to her and her family's delight, was accepted.

It was at college that Penny began to feel for the first time that she came from a socially disadvantaged background. Although on the face of it she had no reason to feel like that - after all, she was bright and well-educated, and had gone to an excellent school - she was suddenly aware of the differences between herself and the other students, who came from upper-class families and had been brought up in the lap of luxury. They had a different mentality and way of speaking, and she felt uncomfortable with them. She was often hurt by her classmates' jibes about her origins. She knew they meant no harm, and that they had been brought up with preconceptions about people who came from her sort of background. She also knew that they admired her intelligence, but they took no pains to conceal their scorn of the "primitive people" who came from Penny's type of town. Penny wanted to bury herself whenever they talked like that and, although she told herself repeatedly that she was not inferior to them, she could not overcome her feelings of inferiority. She began to wallow in them and allow them to dominate her.

When she visited her classmates' homes, she felt that, even with maximum effort, she could never equal their lifestyle. They lived in large houses with well-stocked bookshelves, and culture emanating from every corner. When she went home for a visit, there was always a commotion, with loads of kids all over the place, and never a quiet moment. Loud music blared, and friends and relatives came in and out of her parents' house like a central bus terminal. Penny loved the sounds, smells and atmosphere of her childhood, and she enjoyed her visits. However, each time she left the city to visit her family, the transition became sharper, and this fueled her growing inferiority complex. She never invited friends to her parents' house because she was ashamed of her family. She knew she had no reason to be embarrassed, and resolved to rid herself of her feelings of inferiority. She made an effort to do so, but to no avail.

Penny eventually consulted with a Bach flower remedy practitioner, and the Larch extract she took helped her overcome her feelings of insecurity and inferiority. She realized she had to rely on her own abilities and talents, which were far superior to those of many of her friends. She had to concentrate on her studies and use them as a tool to achieve her goals, which no one could take away from her. She was imbued with new strength and a fighting spirit to show the world who she was and what she was worth. Her belief in her abilities was stronger than ever, and this enhanced her self-image, enabling her to free herself of her former inhibitions. She was sure of herself, and steadfast in her thoughts and opinions. She now knew that no one could outdo her and that no remark could extinguish her rediscovered inner fire and pride.

Difficult Transitions

Lewis was an active child. He did not like activities that involved too much thought and creativity, preferring outdoor games where he could run around and play with his friends. When he was two years old, his parents began to move from place to place, according to his father's current job. They moved to a particular city, staying there one year before moving to another town, followed by another move just one year later, where they finally put down roots. Each time, Lewis had to get to know a new bunch of kids and new kindergarten teachers. The transitions were increasingly difficult for him, and he became undisciplined, insecure and problematic.

Every time he arrived at a new place, he had to adapt to a new group of kids who already knew each other. He always felt an outsider; he had to get used to his new environment and learn the prevalent codes of behavior and mentality. After the third move, he rebelled. He was fed up with sticking to other people's rules and decided that this time, they would have to adjust to him, and not the other way round. He shut himself off. The new group of children he met looked like one solid mass to him and he had no inclination to try to find his way into it. He felt estranged and, as he was only four and a half years old, expressed this in his own way: He became hyperactive and disinterested, and sometimes even reacted violently.

His behavior only intensified the response he evoked from those around him, who wanted to "tame" him. He felt inferior to the others, as if he was abnormal and was incapable of doing what the other kids did. After a while, Lewis was treated with a Bach flower remedy - Larch extract - and he began to rediscover his sense of security. He became less aggressive and more relaxed, and started to participate in the kindergarten activities. He began to feel a part of the place, and it became more important for him to succeed and prove himself. The positive feedback he received encouraged him to keep on trying. He regained his faith in his own abilities, and eventually calmed down. Now other children wanted him to play with them, and it did not take long for him to become one of the leaders. He now wanted to improve and persevere as much as any of the other children.

Extract 11

Elm

Red-Maroon

Aims to change: the temporary feeling of an abnormal burden resulting from a sense of responsibility.

Improves: self-confidence, the ability to bear greater responsibility and to cope better.

Challenging Type

Jim was a tough, courageous and - especially - ambitious guy. He liked going on treks and taking part in adventure sports. He devoted all his resources to activities like trekking, jeep trips, rappelling and white-water rafting. As soon as he reached the peak of one mountain, he looked for the next one to climb. And when he completed one trip around the world, he started planning the next. He devoted his weekends to hiking trips and earned his living as a guide. As soon as he had saved up enough money, he took off for his next foreign destination.

He was completely taken up with trekking and his sports activities and, as he was extremely ambitious, he decided to establish a travel company specializing in adventure sports. It was the first company of its kind in the country, and was an entirely original concept. He invested a fortune in equipment and in establishing links with other companies, and spent whole days and nights planning treks. Setting up the company was very difficult, but Jim was so determined that the company would be the leader in its field that he devoted himself entirely to establishing it.

In the end, Jim established an excellent business that gained a reputation for providing reliable and unique service. However, despite the company's success, both in terms of reputation and financial returns, Jim suffered from a chronic feeling of inner dissatisfaction for no apparent cause. He constantly searched for ways to improve and change things, as he felt that there were better ways of doing them. Even though his staff were dedicated and among the best guides in the country, he still felt there was room for improvement and greater heights of professionalism. The high level of stress generated by the intensive work often brought Jim to breaking point, and he was prone to bad moods which had been completely foreign to him before he set up the company.

When he fell victim to one of these moods, he was tortured by the thought that the company was on the verge of collapse. He would panic and, at times like these, was unapproachable. The members of staff would avoid talking to him, not even to consult with him on urgent matters. When these depressions and anxiety attacks passed, the workers would talk to him frankly, and try to convince him that all was well, and that was no need for him to be uptight and concerned.

When Jim realized that his responses were inappropriate, he decided to take himself in hand in order to regain his former composure and peace of mind. While he knew it was no simple matter to run a business, he had not dreamed that it would have such an effect on him. As he had no intention of closing the company down when it was at the height of its success, he opted for a Bach flower remedy.

He was treated with Elm and Aspen extracts. The Elm extract helped him cope on a day-to-day basis with the great amount of responsibility he had taken on, and he began to feel more in control of what was going on around him; he regained his peace of mind, which enabled him to deal with stressful situations. The tasks involved in running the company, which had seemed impossible to him, were now more manageable.

His former self-confidence in the face of these challenges returned. The Aspen extract enabled him to feel more in touch with reality, and that he could cope with it. He was no longer prone to bad moods, and he continued to run the company successfully.

Born to the Theater

Naomi attended one of the most prestigious acting schools in the country. In time, she became a well-known actress and was in great demand for dramas, comedies and even for TV commercials. She occupied a position of honor in the world of theater and entertainment. She was a perfectionist, with a very high level of self-awareness, and played good roles to great critical acclaim. However, Naomi's self-criticism was so severe that she always found fault with any role she played and thought there was always room for improvement. She was ambitious, always in the running for any role she wanted, and constantly on the look-out for her next role. For years, she was one of the busiest actresses in the country.

However, as time passed and increasing numbers of young actresses filled the successful theater companies, Naomi received fewer parts. When she was not involved in a play, she felt that the public would quickly forget her. This plunged her into depression, and she became susceptible to fears and anxieties. At times like these, Naomi was sure her entire world was about to collapse around her, that she had not chosen the right line of work, and that she did not have the wherewithal to keep up the relentless pace to win roles and remain in the spotlight.

These moods became more frequent, although her situation was not as catastrophic as she imagined. The public still loved her, and she was praised for her acting. The only difference was that it was harder for her to land roles than it had been. Sometimes she felt that this was the end of the world.

Eventually, Naomi realized that there was no reason to go on suffering these depressions and anxiety attacks, and consulted with a Bach flower remedy practitioner. She was treated with Elm extract and felt a tremendous sense of relief right from the start. A feeling of greater self-confidence replaced the depression and distress she had previously experienced. Her fears dissipated, and she felt in control of her life once more; she no longer felt that she had chosen the wrong profession. She knew that she had been born to be an actress. Even if she did not land exactly the part she wanted, and found it harder to get work than in the past, she would deal with the situation differently. She was strong enough to handle it. She would not allow these crises to bring her to the brink of despair. She could cope better and was emotionally prepared to take on the challenges that lay ahead, both in her chosen profession and in life in general.

Extracts for the Treatment of Over-Anxiety

Extract 8*

Chicory

Light Blue

Aims to change: possessiveness (also in relation to other people), demand for respect and obedience, selfishness.

Improves: ability to forego selfish desires by showing concern for others.

Anxious Selfishness

Ray was a strict father, and life with him was not easy for his three sons. He demanded to know about everything they did, and he always insisted that they tell him where they were going, when they would be back, who they were going out with, and so on. His over-involvement in their personal lives did not stop there. He interfered in important life decisions they had to make, ranging from which subject to major in at school, and which college to apply for, to what kind of furniture they should choose for their rooms, and the type of computer they should buy. He never let them think for themselves or express their real wishes. He was always involved in their activities, and made decisions for them, or with them.

Ray's children felt like they were in a prison. Their father's prying eyes followed them everywhere, all the time. They sometimes had to devise convoluted schemes when they wanted to do something without their father's knowledge. Their mother was their accomplice and stood by them over the years. She helped them do things that they knew in advance that their father would not allow them to do, like going on trips with friends or working during vacations to make money.

Ray could not control his relentless prying and his involvement in their lives. Their appeals for him to stop poking his nose into their business fell on deaf ears. He was sure he was doing it for their sakes, out of sincere concern for their welfare, despite the fact that they repeatedly told him that his behavior was in complete contrast with his motives, and that he was being destructive instead of helpful. But Ray stuck to his guns.

When the eldest boy graduated from high school, he decided to go to college. He applied for computer sciences because he had always dreamed of working in that field. Ray, however, insisted that his son's brilliant grades made him eligible for medical school. The shouting matches between them reached high decibels. The two other boys and Ray's wife backed the son, but to no avail. Ray was determined that his son would become a doctor, come what may.

Not even the numerous snide comments that Jim was really thinking of himself rather than his son's good had any effect. They told him that he really wanted his son to fulfill his own dreams, even though his son would be unhappy as a doctor. Ray ignored their comments. In the end, when the son decided unequivocally that he would study computer sciences, Ray saw he had no choice but to threaten not to finance his son's studies. His son knew that if his father carried out his threat, he would not be able to attend college, as he had no other source of funding. With a heavy heart, he applied for pre-med, and was accepted immediately, as his father had predicted.

He began his studies, and hated every moment. The material did not interest him and he increasingly skipped classes and lectures. Ray saw that his son was not interested in his studies and, after much soul-searching, he decided to consent to his son's wishes to apply for computer sciences. Now, however, the son would have to wait until the next academic year, not to mention the money wasted on a whole year's tuition fees.

After receiving his father's permission to study what he really wanted, he was deliriously happy. Ray regretted his insistence on medicine, and gradually realized that his demands had been unreasonable. He was very sorry about what he had done to his son, and resolved to change his ways. He had two other sons, he thought, and he would behave differently with them.

He consulted with a Bach flower remedy practitioner and was treated with Chicory. His obsessive involvement in his sons' lives began to diminish, and he allowed them more leeway. He no longer felt he was doing something wrong when he was not in full control of everything they did. His newfound desire to allow his sons to get on with their lives, and to see them enjoy their freedom, gave him a lot of satisfaction. He started to realize how much he had forced his will on his children and that he had acted extremely selfishly. With this realization, his concern for his sons entered the normal range, and he succeeded in neutralizing his selfishness and his own wishes.

A Void

Donna had got married fairly late in life - at the age of 40 - while her three older sisters had married at a relatively young age. Each one had children, and Donna was a full-time aunt who visited her nephews and nieces whenever she could. She spent each afternoon with a different sister, playing with the kids; she bought them games, toys and candies, and devoted a lot of time and attention to them.

As they grew up, Donna became excessively involved in the lives of her nephews and nieces. When they told her "secrets," she would pass them on to her sisters, and her nephews and nieces gradually realized that she could not be trusted. Donna began to be critical of them. They did not always like what she had to say, and often thought it was none of her business what they did. She felt free to express her opinion about the things they did, the way they did them, and why they should do them differently, and considered it her right to meddle, even though it was not always appropriate.

Over the years, the nephews and nieces began to treat Donna with contempt. After receiving so much attention, love and affection from her, they felt that Donna had become a nuisance. Nothing was sacred, and she would inquire about everything they did, from the subjects they studied at school to their new boyfriend or girlfriend, and what they did when they went out in the evenings. The nephews and nieces started to lose their patience with her and often ignored her when she came to visit. They called her "old maid" and "pest" behind her back. She was very hurt and realized she had to change her behavior. Her sisters had mentioned this to her on several occasions but, despite her will to change, and her attempts to do so, she was unable to change her attitude.

Eventually, she consulted with a Bach flower remedy practitioner for help, and was treated with Chicory. She began to understand that she should be less pushy with other people, and that she should not interfere in their affairs. She reached a high degree of awareness about the interest she took in her nephews and nieces, and understood that it had been a result of her being unmarried, and of her attempt to fill the void by becoming involved in the lives of her sisters' children.

She began to think of other areas of interest to which she could devote some of her time and energies, and she enrolled in some interesting courses. In time, her life was filled with other interests and, when she visited her sisters, she inquired less into the affairs and lives of her nephews and nieces, stopped criticizing them, and displayed her affection and concern for them in other, less pushy, ways. The transformation was considerable and her nephews and nieces now treated her with sincere affection.

Extract 32

Vine

Green

Aims to change: domineering, inflexible, ambitious, strong leadership qualities.

Improves: wisdom, leadership with understanding, strength, acting as a guide and support for others.

The Boss

Mike was a domineering husband with a tyrannical streak. His word was always final, and his wife did not stand a chance against him. Whenever she made a suggestion, he would dismiss it scornfully, and when she had anything to say, he ignored her wishes, as if they were inconsequential. He always showed his wife how he had thought about something beforehand, how right he was, and why things should be done his way.

He was responsible for all their financial affairs. He planned the budget, and knew their current bank balance, what they should spend money on, and when they could afford a vacation, a new electrical appliance, and so on. Because Mike kept tabs on the state of their finances, he was always the one who came up with new ideas, such as a family trip, or a new computer or washing-machine. He had a monopoly on all the big projects - not because his wife was incapable of making such decisions, but because she had no idea what their financial status was.

For his part, he was sure he was doing the maximum for his family. He relied on himself more than on anyone else, and was convinced that he was acting out of devotion to his family. He did not even notice that his wife felt deprived. She felt that he did not respect her sufficiently, or give her the credit she deserved.

While the children were small, Mike's wife was unaware of her husband's domineering attitude. Sometimes, she even felt relieved that she did not have to concern herself with financial matters. She had enough responsibility without that. However, the children eventually grew up and left home, and Mike's wife now had more time for herself. She would go shopping and occasionally buy herself something to wear, spend time in cafés with her friends, and generally enjoy life with fewer daily pressures.

It was then that she began to notice how domineering Mike was. He demanded to know how much money she had spent, when and on what, and with whom she had spent time in cafés. He checked up on her activities every day. As Mike's wife had a cell-phone, it was no problem for Mike to call her several times a day to check what she was doing, with whom, and when she would get home. He found it hard to cope with the freedom his wife had at this stage of their lives. He began to feel he no longer had full control over his domestic affairs, and he found it hard to take.

After a while, his wife reached the end of her tether with her husband's behavior. She felt that if she did not put him in his place, and if he did not change his ways, their marriage would be in jeopardy. She talked to him about it repeatedly, and although he understood her and sincerely wanted to change his nature, he was incapable of doing so. His domineering attitude was innate, and he could not rid himself of it.

Eventually, at the last moment, after his wife had given up, Mike decided to consult with a Bach flower remedy practitioner. He was treated with Vine extract, and the change was immediate. He became more considerate of his wife and others around him, and started showing signs of tolerance and patience. He now listened to others before he said his piece, and took other people's opinions into consideration. Only after reaching the conclusion that he could help the other person, and show them a better way to act, did he try to convince them that he was right. He now found it easier to give his wife some space, and he bothered her less. He understood that he did not have to suffocate a person and get them to account for their every move in order to show how much he sincerely cared for them. Mike and his wife now enjoyed a much happier and more harmonious married life.

Destructive Leadership

Sonia was the head of a women's organization in the town where she lived. She was a born leader with extraordinary charisma, and was always at the forefront wherever she went. In her youth, she had been the leader of her class, and later she was a member of the student union in college. After graduating, she joined the local branch of one of the political parties and became publicly active, until she was finally chosen to head the local women's organization.

Her leadership qualities were unquestioned, and she was a very intelligent and ambitious woman whom the other women followed blindly. However, she had a number of shortcomings. She was a domineering person, and she often criticized and upbraided her subordinates in the organization. She had outbursts of rage that were always unexpected. She could come to work in the morning full of the joys of spring and then, with no prior warning and for no apparent reason, lash out at her subordinates.

She was always convinced that her approach was right, and was not flexible enough to listen to the opinions of the other women in the organization, or to take their ideas into consideration. Her behavior deteriorated over the years, and it became increasingly difficult to work with her. Sometimes things got so bad that she would abuse some of the members of the organization. Ironically, its motto, which called for tolerance, the prevention of violence, and so on, contrasted with her behavior, and it was absurd that someone like Sonia should continue to head it.

The members of the organization decided to remove Sonia from office in the next elections, and that is what happened. After her defeat, Sonia felt that she had a good chance to get her position back in the next elections - but only if she changed her behavior drastically. She was aware of her shortcomings, especially the destructive domineering streak she had in her. She felt that she had gradually become harder over the years, and she had started to behave that way at home with her husband, children and grandchildren.

She decided to take a Bach flower remedy and was treated with Vine extract. She immediately calmed down and began to rediscover her ability to be patient and more tolerant of others - qualities she had forgotten about. She was now able to listen to other people, give of herself, and offer new ideas, not because she wanted to impose her will on others, but as a result of a sincere wish to guide and instruct. She was now able to hold herself in check rather than vent her anger on someone, and she could identify the situations that led to her outbursts. She learned to channel herself into other directions whenever she felt stressed. She now succeeded in achieving her objectives in a pleasant manner and this impacted on others around, both at work and at home.

Sonia won her position back in the following elections, and this time she ran the organization more calmly and in an entirely different atmosphere.

Extract 3

Beech

Pink

Aims to change: intolerance, a tendency to criticize, arrogance, impudence, a judgmental attitude.
Improves: tolerance.

The Terror of the School

Colin was the principal of a high school in an outlying town. In contrast with the recent trend for teachers and principals to relate to the students as their equals and try to be like their friends/colleagues, he terrorized them. Colin was a strict principal from the "old school." He was older than most people in his position, and believed in strict education and clearly defined boundaries for the students. Sometimes he "persecuted" the students by repeatedly investigating their every move if there had been an incident at school. He made them feel that he was everywhere, watching from the side. They felt threatened.

Long years of service as a principal had left their mark on Colin. Many years earlier, at the beginning of his career, he had displayed tolerance and patience with the students, but he had lost that ability in recent years. He became an unpleasant person to be with, not just as a principal. The teachers spoke to him only when it was absolutely necessary, and then only about school matters. He was not a congenial conversationalist, and he was very critical of the teachers at the school, the Department of Education, and modern methods of education. The teachers had to tread warily and find a middle ground between the current approach to teaching as laid down by Department regulations, and Colin's beliefs.

Colin gradually became an intolerable person to be with. Everyone avoided coming into contact with him, and the most menacing phrase any teacher could use - and it was readily adopted by the teachers - was: "I'll send you to the principal," something that never ended well. The regional school inspector, who was Colin's superior, received numerous complaints about him from teachers and parents of students alike. The inspector summoned Colin to come see her, and she spelled out the situation to him. Colin realized that he had to do something to change his behavior if he wanted to retain his position at the school. He deeply regretted that the situation had deteriorated to the point where the school inspector had been compelled to speak to him. He resolved to become calmer and more patient by taking a Bach flower remedy.

Colin received intensive treatment with Beech extract. He took the drops several times a day, and the change in him was rapid. He began to relate to the students with respect and patience, allowed them to express their opinions, and took their ideas into consideration. He began to treat the teachers completely differently, and often spent time with them just chatting about trivial things. He even smiled occasionally. The teachers felt he was mellowing, and they now found it easier to consult with him and discuss current issues. The students no longer feared him after they saw their friends leaving Colin's office in a relaxed manner, not in tears or in a state of shock. The entire atmosphere at the school changed for the better, with Colin being the main beneficiary. He was now perceived quite differently and the students no longer considered him as their foe, but rather as someone they could talk to about any problem. That had never happened before. Colin now knew that he was on the correct path.

Inner Filth

Miriam had been abused by her husband for 25 intolerable years. He humiliated her verbally, insulted her, oppressed her, and treated her like dirt. But his main thing was abusing her physically by beating her violently. When he got into a frenzy, he would punch her, hit her with a belt, throw heavy things at her head, and even attack her with a hammer. On several occasions, she ended up in the intensive care unit. Many times she was only inches from death, but her complaints to the police were useless. Even when her husband had been removed from the house by police injunctions, he always came back eventually, and the abuse would start all over again.

One day, after an attack, Miriam went berserk. She grabbed a large kitchen knife, ran up to her husband, stabbed him in the heart three times until she had no more strength left, and saw him collapse and die in front of her. She was sentenced to seven years' imprisonment after the judge took the tragic circumstances of the killing into account. She expressed regret over the incident, but although she felt a tremendous sense of relief that her nightmare was over, she felt that there was something impure deep inside her. When she had done her time, she did not feel that she could start her life all over again as if nothing had happened. Although she knew that she had paid her dues to society, and that she was now free to do as she wished, her emotions permitted her no rest. Her talks with a psychologist helped alleviate her condition, but not sufficiently.

Miriam decided to undergo treatment with a Bach flower remedy, and she was treated over a long period of time with a low dosage of Beech extract. In time, she started to feel that the sense of inner impurity was decreasing and was being replaced by a good, pleasant feeling of wishing to live in harmony with her surroundings and with the people with whom she came into contact. Basic questions which had previously troubled her, such as her role on Earth, what good she could bring to the world after committing murder, and so on, now gave way to questions of a much more positive nature, like: "What can I do today to improve things around me?"; "How can I get involved in positive and constructive activities?"; "What can I do for others so that I can feel better about myself?"

Her philosophy of life changed unrecognizably, and she managed to break out of her shell and start building a new, more successful life for herself in which she could feel satisfaction and inner purity.

Extract 27

Rock Water

White/Light Blue

Aims to change: self-denial, stress, a tendency to set an example, rigidity, a tendency to be pedantic, hypocrisy, suppression and denial of emotions.

Improves: the ability to maintain ideals and flexibility of thought, the ability to benefit from life experience in a relaxed manner.

Getting Better

Ben's parents were political refugees, and he grew up under an ever-present cloud of the horrific experiences his parents had undergone in their country of birth. Ben's father often woke up in the middle of the night petrified with fear, while his mother's emotional scars manifested themselves in her stinginess. She skimped on everything, particularly on food, and lived appallingly ascetically.

Ben's parents had been well-educated professionals in their home country, but worked at relatively menial jobs in their adoptive country. They always encouraged him to study, to get a college degree, and to work in a respectable profession. The most important thing for them was that Ben should make the most of his opportunity as a native of the country, to realize his potential to the full, and to give free rein to his talents. Their sense of having missed the boat themselves was so strong that the atmosphere in their house was charged with their powerful desire to push their son so that he would be successful. They did not mind if it meant him having to leave home, as long as he made a life for himself where they had failed.

For his part, Ben felt the burden of his parents' great

expectations, and he did not want to let them down. He became ambitious to the point of exaggeration, doing everything he could to be top of his class and to get the highest grades, to be the most outstanding sportsman in his age group, and to be the best scout, even if he had to invest long hours in preparation and training in order to succeed. He never gave up. His reward came when his teachers and instructors pointed him out as a model student. He was, of course, a hero among the boys and greatly admired by the girls. He graduated from college with high grades, and was accepted to law school. After graduation and internship, he started to work in a successful law firm in a big city, and became one of the top divorce lawyers in the country. His parents, meanwhile, were so proud of him that they did not mind in the least that he no longer lived with them.

Ben may have become a successful attorney, but the price he had paid was heavy. Because of the mad race to prove himself, and the fact that he had been so hard, demanding and critical with himself, he no longer knew how to enjoy himself, or to take vacations in order to relieve the tensions of his daily existence. He thought that was a waste of time. He did not allow himself to enjoy the small things in life that make everything more pleasant. For example, he refused to buy certain electrical appliances, such as a drier, claiming that they were unnecessary. He did not go out much in the evenings, to movies or cafés. He lived a quite Spartan life, which, in his profession, was a stumbling-block.

He kept up a crazy pace of work, as he always needed to prove he could do even better. So he never took time out to draw breath. The only time he rested was on Sunday, when he would collapse onto the bed and spend most of his time sleeping. Eventually he reached breaking-point and felt that if he did not loosen up, he would collapse. A friend advised him to take a Bach flower remedy. Ben began to take Rock Water extract, which enabled him to slow down the pace without feeling guilty. He started taking things more easily and was less hard on himself. He began to enjoy longer lunch breaks, and to take care of himself; he felt comfortable with his new course of action. Not only did the world not come to an end, but he felt his strength being restored, and found it easier to deal with the routine difficulties of work. He became a calm, relaxed person who could maintain flexibility of thought and was less rigid with himself and those around him.

Inferiority Complex

Gloria always thought she was less successful than other people, despite the fact that she was not only a very talented person, but always succeeded to a much greater extent than she expected. She was always surprised when she succeeded - she sincerely believed that she would fail in every mission she took upon herself, regardless of the number of times she succeeded and proved to herself that the opposite was true. She was black and had grown up in a white neighborhood. Her confidence diminished when she was old enough to realize that she was different from the other students in her class. This was in spite of the fact that, besides certain dishes that the students ate at home, there were no differences between her and her classmates. However, she felt inferior to them. On the one hand, she wanted to show them she was just as good as they were, and she tried to be the best and to set an example. On the other, regardless of how hard she tried and how hard she worked, she always thought the others, with their white skins, were more successful than she was.

It was her inferiority complex which spurred her on to become independent and establish a successful advertising company. But she was a tough nut, fastidious and strict, with an obsessive preoccupation with details. This actually had a bad effect on her company, and talented and diligent employees left the company because of Gloria's obsession. She gained a reputation in the field as being a tough employer. She was certain that she had failed again and that her talent was inadequate. It was only after her husband had made an enormous effort to convince her not to give up that she realized she had to deal with her conflicting feelings, and she decided to try a Bach flower remedy.

She was treated with Rock Water extract, and became calmer and less strict both with herself and with her employees. She began to feel less stressed out and found it easier to assess herself objectively. She was no longer so obsessive about being the best at all costs, and accepted the fact that not everything in life would work out exactly as she planned. She should accept her failures with equanimity. Gloria could now live with herself more easily and compromise on less-than-perfect results.

Extract 31*

Vervain

Brilliant White

Aims to change: excessive enthusiasm, fanaticism, excessive energy leading to over-exertion and emotional stress, anger at injustice.

Improves: peace of mind, confidence in self-control, liberal thought.

Life Can Be Different

Peter grew up in a religious home. He had four siblings, and his father was a firm believer in applying the proverbial "rod." He brought his children up strictly, and truly believed that by beating them and punishing them he was giving them a superb upbringing. Not only would they follow the straight and narrow path, he thought, but they would also learn to fear and respect him.

When Peter became a parent himself, he treated his own children the same way. He believed that that was the way to raise children. He remembered how he and his brothers had feared and respected their father, and how his father had been a man of his word. He loved his children dearly and was terrified that they may get into bad company, because that would be on his conscience. He considered this to be the correct way to bring up his children. His wife, on the other hand, thought exactly the opposite, and vehemently opposed the use of any form of corporal punishment for raising children.

Peter and his wife had loud arguments. Their children heard their disagreements, and naturally sided with their mother. This made Peter even angrier. "Don't tell me how to bring up the children. They're my children as well," he shouted at her. Meanwhile, she would retort: "They'll only hate you for this. Children aren't raised like that anymore." There were endless arguments. Often, when Peter was angry with one of the children and raised his hand, his wife would protect the child and not allow Peter to hit him. "Over my dead body," she would say, and he would back down until his next outburst of anger. He did not strike his wife, as he respected her too much. Although he attached great importance to whatever she said, he could not bring himself to adopt her "modern" approach to child-rearing because it went against the grain of all the values that had been instilled into him as a child.

In her distress, and out of fear for their marriage, Peter's wife persuaded him to try a Bach flower remedy. She believed it could enlighten him and change his attitude toward the subject. She was right. Peter was treated with a Vervain extract and, after an initial intensive treatment, his attitude became more flexible, and he began to open up to new, unfamiliar ideas.

He was now amazingly receptive, and his wife could hardly believe the extent of the transformation that had come over him. Peter became more relaxed and gained a greater degree of self-control. It seemed as if he had learned to count to ten before having an angry or violent outburst. He eventually admitted that there might be another way of raising the children, and stopped adhering blindly to the only way he believed in. In times of crisis, he encouraged the children to tell him what it was that was bothering them, and why they behaved in the way they did. He sincerely looked for a new approach, and discovered that not only was there another way to bring up children, but the new way was better and more effective. Most importantly, his children no longer feared him and were not afraid of telling the truth, even if it was difficult. Peter felt like a new man, and was very proud of the progress he had made, from "the world of darkness to the world of light," as he put it.

Never Give Up

Stan was one of the "old guard." He was not fond of change and, when the first fast-food restaurant was built in his village, he got a group of people his age to protest against the "intruder." His family had lived in the village for generations, and he objected to any change in their peaceful existence. But the younger generation was in favor of the new development plans for the village, which included the construction of office buildings and a number of new roads. Stan was enraged by the very thought that the young people in the village wanted to change his entire environment.

He knew, however, that something had to be done to keep the younger generation in the village, otherwise his generation would die out and the village would become a ghost town after the younger lot left for the jobs and the bright lights of the city. He was "the last of the Mohicans," and the arguments he waged with the younger residents did not exactly do wonders for his health, which left a lot to be desired. Stan eventually realized he would have to accept the modern developments, but an old trooper like him could not give up the fight so easily. His daughter saw the struggle he was having with himself and referred him to a Bach flower remedy practitioner for treatment. He was treated with Vervain, and the initial impact it had on Stan was that he no longer flew off the handle when "sensitive" subjects were discussed. He now found to easier to stay calm while the village changed and became more modern. Despite his advanced years, Stan became a more open person and attained a flexibility of thought which he had never previously had, even when he was a young man. Towards the end of his life, he became more tranquil, and was sorry that he had not taken the Bach remedy years earlier. Life now seemed easier and more pleasant for Stan.

THE LIST

Extracts for the Treatment of Fears

Extracts for the Treatment of Insecurity

Extracts for the Treatment of Apathy (Detachment from Reality)

LIST OF BACH'S FLOWERS, IN NUMERICAL ORDER

 1. Agrimony*
 2. Aspen
 3. Beech
 4. Centaury*
 5. Cerato*
 6. Cherry Plum
 7. Chestnut Bud
 8. Chicory*
 9. Clematis*
10. Crab Apple
11. Elm
12. Gentian*
13. Gorse
14. Heather
15. Holly
16. Honeysuckle
17. Hornbeam
18. Impatiens*
19. Larch
20. Mimulus*
21. Mustard
22. Oak
23. Olive
24. Pine
25. Red Chestnut
26. Rock Rose*
27. Rock Water
28. Scleranthus*
29. Star of Bethlehem
30. Sweet Chestnut
31. Vervain*
32. Vine
33. Walnut
34. Water Violet*
35. White Chestnut
36. Wild Oat
37. Wild Rose
38. Willow